Butterflies Be Gone

A Hands-On Approach to Sweat-Proof Public Speaking

Arthur H. Bell, Ph.D.

New York   Chicago   San Francisco   Lisbon   London   Madrid   Mexico City
Milan   New Delhi   San Juan   Seoul   Singapore   Sydney   Toronto

The McGraw·Hill Companies

Library of Congress Cataloging-in-Publication Data

Bell, Arthur H. (Arthur Henry), 1946–.
    Butterflies be gone : a hands-on approach to sweat-proof public speaking / by
Arthur H. Bell.
       p.   cm.
    ISBN 0-07-147362-9 (alk. paper)
    1. Public speaking.   I. Title.

   PN4129.15.B46   2007
   808.5′1—dc22   2007037609

1 2 3 4 5 6 7 8 9 10 11 12 13 14 15 16 17 18 19 20   DOC/DOC   0 9 8

ISBN 978-0-07-147362-0
MHID   0-07-147362-9

McGraw-Hill books are available at special quantity discounts to use as premiums and
sales promotions or for use in corporate training programs. To contact a representative,
please visit the Contact Us pages at www.mhprofessional.com.

Important Disclaimer:

The author is a speech coach who has worked with thousands of professional men and
women. He is not a medical or psychological practitioner. No medical or psychological
advice or counsel is intended in this book for any individual reader. Anyone experiencing
physical or emotional symptoms associated with speech anxiety should seek the services
of a health professional as an important first step toward resolving these issues.

This book is printed on acid-free paper.

Dedicated to my daughter in college, Lauren E. Bell.
Speaker's nerves never had a chance against her.

Contents

Preface

NOTHING MATTERS MORE to your success as a speaker than your comfort in front of an audience. If speaker's nerves have interrupted that comfort (to put it mildly), do something about it. Speaker's nerves, in case you haven't met the beast head-on, is the common but frightening experience of physical and emotional distress aroused by public speaking occasions. Figure out, with the help of these pages, what you are experiencing and what you can do to make public presentations an opportunity to shine, not to shake.

My interest in speaker's nerves grew from my ongoing work as a speech coach with hundreds of managers, executives, and other professionals, including CEOs, congressional representatives, military leaders, and nonprofit executives. All wanted to perform well, for themselves and their organizations, in speeches, media appearances, and convention addresses. In our work together, they came to an important personal discovery: their power as presenters depended on their ability to get real — to be themselves — with their audience. No amount of coaching on eye contact, gestures, movement, and the rest could do much until they found ways to calm down and share themselves with listeners. The energy and excitement we all feel in front of an audience should never be wasted on the short circuit of speaker's nerves.

Gathered here are solutions for the problem of speaker's nerves, with anecdotes, cases, and personal stories from men and women like you who have wrestled with the dragon and found the right sword to slay it. For obvious reasons of privacy, their names and identifying information have been changed. Their stories have been retold with details fictionalized for brevity and readability. Any resemblance to real individuals, events, companies, or circumstances is purely coincidental.

Important Disclaimer: The author is a speech coach who has worked with thousands of professional men and women. He is not a medical or psychological practitioner. No medical or psychological advice or counsel is intended in this book for any individual reader. Anyone experiencing physical or emotional symptoms associated with speech anxiety should seek the services of a health professional as an important first step toward resolving these issues.

Acknowledgments

I OWE AN enormous debt of gratitude to the hundreds of managers, executives, and other professionals I've worked with as a speech coach. In particular, my heartfelt appreciation goes to business leaders who encourage clear, confident speaking at IBM, Cisco Systems, American Stores, Citibank, TRW, Sun Microsystems, Apple, Wells Fargo, Williamsburg Foundation, Safeway, Santa Fe Railway, Franklin Templeton, SNP Communications, New York Life, Deutsche Telekom, Cushman Wakefield, the U.S. Navy, the U.S. State Department, Cost Plus World Market, Bank of America, VISA, British Telecom, AT&T, and China Resources. My colleagues for the last decade at the Masagung Graduate School of Management, University of San Francisco, have been generous in sharing their expertise and friendship, as have former colleagues at Georgetown University and the University of Southern California. Special thanks go to Mike Duffy, Dean of the School of Business and Management at USF, for his encouragement and support. As always, my students at the undergraduate, MBA, and Executive MBA levels have shared their thoughts and lives with me. I thank each of them and no doubt have learned more than I have taught. Among the many medical professionals who lent insight to this book, I want to thank two in particular: James Gardner, M.D., my valued friend and coauthor on two previous books (*Phobias and How to Overcome Them*, and *Overcoming Anxiety, Panic, and Depression*, both published by Career Press); and David Brody, M.D., psychiatrist, who shared profound insights into anxiety and other forms of nervous distress. Portions of medical discussions in this book are based in part on work the author copublished with James Gardner, M.D., including passages that are reprinted, with permission of the publisher, from *Phobias and How to Overcome Them* © 2005 James Gardner, M.D., and Arthur H. Bell, Ph.D. Published by Career Press, Franklin Lakes, NJ; 800-227-3371. All rights reserved.

The Speaker's Personality Instrument (SPI) in Appendix B is based on the author's personality instrument from *Winning with Difficult People*, third edition, by Arthur H. Bell and Dayle M. Smith. Copyright © 2003 by Barron's Educational Series. Reprinted by arrangement with Barron's Educational Series, Inc., Hauppauge, NY.

My editors at McGraw-Hill, especially Karen S. Young and Jenn Tust, were virtual saints not only for their commitment to this project and extraordinary expertise but also for their patience with its author. I also extend heartfelt thanks once again to my friend and the best literary agent in the world, Grace Freedson, of Grace Freedson Publishing Network, for her faith in me and in this project. Finally, I thank my wife, partner, and colleague Dayle Smith for her counsel, ideas, and love.

Introduction

Welcome to the world of speaker's nerves. I assume you want to leave as quickly as possible. If you are truly unfamiliar with speaker's nerves, let me introduce you. Speaker's nerves is a complicated bundle of physical and emotional symptoms stirred up by public speaking opportunities.

About 40 percent of American adults, according to a recent Gallup poll, suffer from a fear of public speaking. Comedian Jerry Seinfeld spoke for them when he quipped that, at a funeral, mourners would rather be in the grave than giving the eulogy. Fear of public speaking regularly ranks as fear number one, even ahead of the fear of death, in large-scale surveys summed up in the *Book of Lists* (2007).

The fact that so many of us are stewing over speaker's nerves doesn't make the experience any more comfortable. In this case, misery doesn't love company. No one feels more alone in the universe than the sweating, palpitating, gasping speaker who just wants to get to the end of the speech, crawl into a hole, and die of embarrassment.

For some, speaker's nerves are a minor annoyance—a speed bump on the freeway of life. For others, the fear of public speaking looms like a storm cloud over their personal and professional lives, threatening careers and even relationships. Countless thousands of talented men and women have reluctantly said "no thanks" to promotions because the new jobs entailed additional speaking responsibilities. Famous politicians, actors, and musicians (Winston Churchill, Laurence Olivier, Barbra Streisand, Kim Basinger, and many others) have fought back against performance fears that once endangered their careers.

Seinfeld notwithstanding, the experience of speaker's nerves is no laughing matter. This book offers practical help in a seven-part plan:

1. A thorough description of the symptoms of speaker's nerves, including narratives from sufferers

2. An explanation, in lay terms, of the brain and body events that help account for speaker's nerves

3. Case histories showing how, when, and why speaker's nerves plagued the careers of professional people in a variety of fields—and how they fought back successfully against their fears

4. A chapter filled with practical solutions for speaker's nerves, a virtual trunk show of tried-and-true remedies from which you can choose ways to end your speech anxiety

5. Guidance on how to involve your doctor in your recovery strategy

6. A planning guide so your good intentions don't evaporate, because you have the opportunity to write down exactly what you are going to do about speaker's nerves and then measure your progress

7. A Speaker's Personality Instrument that reveals personal characteristics and preferences that may make you more vulnerable to speaker's nerves and suggests ways to cope.

Can you put speaker's nerves behind you once and for all? You're holding this book in your hands, and it's not shaking. That's a start. The journey to confident, enjoyable speaking continues with Chapter 1.

1

The Experience of Speaker's Nerves

WHAT DOES AN attack of speaker's nerves feel like?

If you're holding this book, you probably know at least one answer to that question: your own vivid memories of encounters with the beast. Few readers turn to a book on speaker's nerves with only a spectator's interest in mind. They either are bedeviled by speaker's nerves themselves or are trying to help a loved one, friend, or coworker who suffers from speech anxiety.

This chapter will help you understand the complex but common experience of speaker's nerves more thoroughly. You have probably wondered, "Do others experience what I experience? Does someone else really know how bad it feels? Is it all in my head? And if so, why can't I shake it?"

You may also wonder if you need medical or psychological help to properly diagnose and treat your speaker's nerves. It's highly recommended that you discuss your symptoms and feelings with your doctor and/or mental health professional, if only to rule out any underlying conditions that may be contributing to your speech anxiety.

In reviewing the most common symptoms of speaker's nerves, we run the risk of arousing fears more than quieting them. (This phenomenon can be observed at medical schools, where doctors-in-training often convince themselves that they are in fact ill with whatever disease or condition they are studying at the time.) Don't let the following descriptions, quite vivid and personal at times, prey upon your emotions as you get ready for your next presentation. The purpose of describing common symptoms here is not to scare you but instead to remind you that countless others have felt what you have suffered through—and have prevailed as confident, enthusiastic presenters. You may also find some solace in finding a clear description of the physical and emotional sensations you've felt: "Yes, that's exactly what it was like!"

A Practical Approach to Speaker's Nerves

We begin our description of speaker's nerves in a pragmatic, practical way. A follow-on chapter then provides a scientific, physiological description and explanation of the same nervous syndrome. At the outset, we need to say a few words about the value of each approach.

The pragmatic description of speaker's nerves (what it feels like "on the ground") has priority here because that description rings most true to speakers. After all, as we rise to speak, none of us is conscious of our synapses firing, our glands discharging chemical signals, or our nerve pathways coursing with energy. Although these underlying physical phenomena are real in the sense that they happen, they are not "real" in the way that upsets us most: perspiration plinking off our nose, heart beating wildly, hands quivering, knees shaking. That's "real" to someone suffering from speaker's nerves, and it's there that we must begin.

Pragmatism concerns itself not with what you *should* feel as a speaker nor with what is rational or logical in a speaking circumstance ("Don't be silly. There's nothing to be afraid of"), but instead with what you *do* feel. This approach, advanced by the early-twentieth-century philosopher William James, pays attention to physical and emotional sensations even when they do not fit into popular theories and hypotheses. "What is the problem, and what can we do about it?" are typical Jamesian questions in dealing with any area of human experience, including speaker's nerves.

At the other extreme of explanation are the scientific theories of physiology, dealt with in detail in Chapter 7, which attempts to account for speaker's nerves by reference to an elaborate interplay of electrochemical impulses within the body. Especially because these explanations try to describe what goes on in the human brain and the rest of the central nervous system during fear and anxiety states, they are extraordinarily complicated (interestingly so) and subject to frequent revision and even revolution as we learn more about how these still-mysterious systems work.

Knowing Why Can Help

Why bother with complex physiological theories at all? First, we can satisfy our curiosity by knowing as much as possible about the deep causes of a nervous phenomenon that perplexes and bedevils us. Second, we can understand more thoroughly the hows and whys of the broad range of solutions, interventions, pharmacological aids (tranquilizers, antidepressants, and other "mood medicines"), and talk therapy, including desensitization and psychoanalysis.

But most important, some knowledge of the physiology behind speaker's nerves can help us say, "These sensations are not totally in my control, nor can I rely on ordinary willpower to make them go away." Although we may often feel frustrated that we can't "flip the switches" of our internal chemistry by our conscious will, we can also be relieved in a way that the body, above all in its nervous system, has such superb alarms, energizing mechanisms, and survival responses when it perceives its well-being to be threatened. It comes as a relief, in other words, to discover that a bout with speaker's nerves "isn't my fault" any more than a headache or a bad dream. The onset of speaker's nerves is quite similar to the weather: you can go for long stretches without a cloud in the sky, so to speak, and then experience a period of blustery storms. The goal is not to make the weather go away, any more than we can exert absolute control over our moods, anxieties, and fears. Instead, the goal is to predict the "weather" when possible and prepare for our comfort and effectiveness in spite of it.

If we could control the specific symptoms of nervousness, we would quickly regret that ability. Surely none of us would wish to be in moment-by-moment, conscious control of, say, the regular beating of our hearts or the digestive actions of our stomachs. We are content to let the vast majority of our body's physiological processes happen by themselves, as it were, in accordance with a sophisticated system that we have just begun to understand. In short, the more we know about the physiology of speaker's nerves, the more we may decide to cut ourselves some slack by allowing those responses, like the weather, simply to happen—and, in doing so, to gain freedom from our fearfulness about them.

Symptoms of Speaker's Nerves

In our discussion, we will show the various ways in which speaker's nerves are experienced by real people. The following list is not intended to be exhaustive. You or someone you know may have a symptom that does not appear here. But it's almost certain that, among these specific descriptions of what speaker's nerves feel like, you will find one or more that coincides with your own experiences. That discovery alone can be reassuring: "Someone else has felt what I'm going through! I'm not alone in these awful and painful feelings."

Although listed separately, these nervous sensations rarely appear as discrete feelings. Sufferers often find that the experience of speaker's nerves combines several of these feelings simultaneously or, just as likely, arranges them in a sequential order of rising and falling emotions ("first I feel nausea, then I feel weak in the knees, then my hands begin to tremble," and so forth).

Some symptoms of speaker's nerves, such as excessive perspiration and jitteriness, can be observed; other symptoms can't be seen, including feelings of dread and panic, mental lapses, and feelings of extreme embarrassment. Whether obvious to others or simply felt by the speaker, the symptoms can be annoying and frightening. If left unattended, they can turn into recurring barriers to confident, enjoyable presenting.

No reader of this book should automatically assume that his or her symptoms are solely attributable to speaker's nerves. It's highly recommended that you discuss your symptoms with your physician and/or mental health professional. Our purpose in describing symptoms in detail in this chapter is to clarify sensations that you may recall only through a haze, given the panicky feelings that often accompany speaker's nerves.

Feelings of Dread

Richard S., a banker in the Northwest: "There's no one symptom that I experience with speaker's nerves. Instead, it's more like a cloud of gloom and dread that settles over me as soon as I learn that I have to give a major presentation. That cloud descends like a thick, choking fog as the presentation date gets close. My wife says I mope around the house and look like I just lost my best friend. Inside I feel a mixture of depression and hopelessness, probably akin to finding out you have a terminal disease. Nothing sounds good when a presentation looms. If I go out to dinner or to a movie, I feel like I'm just going through the motions. The dreaded event is always there somewhere in my mind, even when I'm not consciously thinking about it."

Feelings of dread such as those experienced by Richard can occur days or even weeks before the speaking occasion. These feelings can steadily increase as the date nears, or they can come and go as waves of emotion felt particularly during moments of fatigue or when the mind isn't occupied with something else. The experience of dread can rarely be reduced to exact physical feelings such as nausea or headaches. In fact, people plagued by dread associated with speaking often express the wish that they could experience overt symptoms instead of free-floating anxiety and unnamed emotions of despair: "If I had a specific symptom, I could go to the doctor and get it fixed!" one speaker says. "But how do you describe dread? How do you tell someone I just feel scared and very, very sad to my core? And even if I could do it, what could my doctor do to help me?" (As in this case, many people assume that their personal physicians limit their practice to quick visits, short conversations, and prescriptions for pills. Those who feel dread associated with speaking decide in advance that their physicians can't help them.)

For some people, when they are under the influence of adrenaline, clouds of dread have a way of parting just before or during a speech. "I'm

OK once I actually get started," one speaker says. "But I dread giving a presentation right up to the moment I look out at the audience and start to speak." Other speakers experience dread even more intensely during their speaking. They look as if they are having a miserable time, as reflected in their downcast eyes, monotone voice, and rigid posture.

Finally, feelings of dread can extend well beyond the presentation, no matter how well it went in the eyes of the audience. "Everyone said I did just fine," a speaker confides, "but I just can't shake feelings of utter mortification after a speaking occasion. I think of slips I made or things I forgot to say. I think of how nervous I felt and what the audience must have thought of me. I dismiss any praise that I receive as just a pitying effort on the part of audience members to be kind. These feelings gradually fade with time, but I have to admit that when I think of speeches I gave even a couple of years ago, I go through waves of self-loathing all over again."

Feelings of Panic

Brenda Y., an insurance broker in the South: "Even though I know I had a panic attack, I still have trouble describing exactly what it felt like during my last speaking experience. I was about a minute into my speech, when all of a sudden, I felt completely overwhelmed by emotions of fright. I knew I had to get out of there, no matter what, much like a person caught in a stuck elevator. I don't know what it looked like from the outside, but I felt inside as if I were going crazy. My vision got hazy, and I didn't know if I was going to faint or explode. It was undoubtedly the worst feeling I've experienced in my entire life. I mumbled something into the microphone about 'Sorry, I'm feeling ill' and rushed away from the podium to the women's restroom. Later, when I talked to my doctor about the experience, I had difficulty pointing to any one thing that was horrible. I didn't have a specific pain. I couldn't point to anything I was afraid of. But I hope I never have to repeat that moment, and I will avoid public speaking entirely if the price I have to pay for speaking is continued panic attacks."

The panic experience is different from feelings of dread, although dread may certainly follow from a panic attack, as in Brenda's case. Panic comes on as a storm of emotions, often in a matter of seconds. Dread is a

simmering pot of feelings that percolates slowly and steadily at one's emotional core. The specific symptoms of a panic attack include rapid and
sometimes irregular heartbeat, increased rate of breathing, excessive perspiration, shakiness, dry mouth, and nausea. But people who experience
panic attacks usually do not mention these physical sensations as their primary impression and memory of the attack. Like Brenda, they point to a
frightening crescendo of inner emotions and alarms, an unforgettable feeling that can last anywhere from several seconds to several minutes before
beginning to recede. "It's the feeling you get when you suddenly have to
slam on your brakes to avoid a traffic accident," one panic sufferer says,
"but it lasts longer and comes on stronger."

Feelings of Suffocation

Victoria C., a college student in New York: "I think my first experience
with breathing problems occurred when I had to give a two-minute presentation in my public speaking class as a freshman in college. I felt myself
breathing faster and faster, almost panting, as I approached the podium.
It was like I was underwater and couldn't come up for air. I would say a
few words and then gasp for air. Somehow I got through my speech, but
I felt like I was literally dying up there, not to mention the embarrassment
of looking and sounding like a freak. Right after class, I went to the university health center and told a doctor I had had an asthma attack of some
kind. She examined me and said it was probably 'just nerves.' Since I had
never experienced anything like this before, I found it hard to believe that
nerves would make me feel I was suffocating."

People have various ways of describing their feelings of breathlessness: "breathing erratically, taking several quick breaths and then not
breathing at all for a long moment"; "taking huge breaths in and then letting them out, almost like sighing"; "shallow, fast breaths just in my upper
chest"; "letting out all my breath as I spoke and then having to pause to
take a few deep breaths in order to continue"; and "talking just as fast as
I could to get through the speech before feelings of suffocation overwhelmed me—it feels like a race between my speaking and my amount
of oxygen."

These feelings typically begin a few moments before the speech and rapidly intensify in the first thirty seconds or so of speaking. For some speakers, the feelings crest after a minute or two, and then they experience more natural feelings of breathing comfort for the remainder of the speech. Other speakers experience episodes of breathlessness at unpredictable moments, particularly when giving a longer presentation. For most speakers, the sensation of suffocation eases immediately after the presentation ends, but it is not uncommon to see an occasional speaker have to leave the room right after concluding a speech. "I need to get out of the room to catch my breath," one speaker says. "If I stay at the front of the room, I feel everyone's eyes on me. I feel like I have to look like I'm breathing normally. But what I need to do, desperately, is to get it back together by gasping for air, usually in the hallway with my hands on my knees."

Cold, Numb, or Tingling Sensations

Bernard M., a city council member in Florida: "It starts about five minutes before I have to go up and speak. My hands turn ice-cold, even if I rub them together under the table. I feel a kind of pinprick sensation starting at first in my fingertips and then working up to my palms and wrists. The same feelings happen to my toes and feet, which are also frigid by this time. When I actually rise to speak, the tingliness extends to my cheeks and lips. Moving my lips to pronounce words becomes awkward, like trying to talk after you have been outdoors in subzero weather. My lips feel thick and seem to move only in slow motion. I stumble over a lot of my words and have trouble speaking clearly. The cold and tingling feeling can last for several minutes after I'm done speaking. There seems to be nothing I can do to make it go away either when I'm speaking or immediately afterward. It bugs the heck out of me and makes me avoid many speaking opportunities."

The "tingling feeling" can also be felt at times on the upper chest and stomach area. The sensation is described as roughly similar to the feeling in your hand or foot as circulation comes back into it after being "asleep" (numb) from some kind of pressure on the blood supply, for example, sitting cross-legged for a period of time. The sensation of tingles associated with speaker's nerves is not painful but can certainly be irritating and distracting. Although nothing can usually be seen from the outside on the tingling cheek or fingers, many speakers are convinced that their internal irritation over these feelings is obvious to the audience—in effect, that the audience can tell that the speaker is in significant discomfort.

Skin Blotches

Christina R., a cosmetics executive in California: "I have always believed, along with a lot of experts, that one's visual presentation of self is at least as important as the verbal content of a speech. How you look really matters. That's why I get so upset by bright red blotches, some as big as a plum, that appear on my cheeks, neck, and upper chest when I give a speech. They're not there five minutes before the speech (I've checked). But they certainly come out into full bloom within the first minute or so of speaking. And they last for quite a while—sometimes an hour or so—after the speech. So not only am I embarrassed to look like a rose-cheeked clown when I'm speaking, but I also continue to look that way when I'm shaking hands and talking to important people right after the speech. Believe me, this is not the kind of thing the right makeup will cover. These are flame-red blotches, as if someone had slapped me across the cheek. They aren't even symmetrical. The blotch that shows up on my left cheek is twice as large as the blotch on my right cheek. One is shaped like an oval, the other a ragged triangle."

What one speaker accepts as normal and unremarkable, another speaker—Christina, in this case—looks upon as horrific. Men and women alike are susceptible to blotching, with fair-haired and light-skinned people much more likely to notice its presence. The vast majority of speakers experience a rosier complexion when they speak, but this general glow of exercise cannot be mistaken for blotching—one or more well-defined patches, ranging from the size of a quarter to that of a dollar bill or larger. Some blotching is progressive, beginning on the upper cheek early in the speech and growing to include the side or front of the throat as the speech progresses, particularly if the speaker becomes flustered (often by the realization that blotches have appeared again). The blotches are no warmer to the touch than ordinary skin and in most cases are no more sensitive. Less commonly, blotches can appear on the backs of the hands and the inside of the arms, particularly between the wrist and elbow.

Heart Palpitations

Benson P., a furniture salesman in Texas: "I'm an amateur runner, so I'm familiar with the feeling of my heart when it beats fast and hard. In fact, my coach has us take our pulses at various times during a run to check on our levels of conditioning. But what I feel from my heart when I run is nothing like the sledgehammer pounding I experience a few minutes before I begin to speak. On several speaking occasions, this sensation didn't let up. I tried to take deep breaths to lower my pulse, and I tried to relax. But nothing worked. I was so worried after one such presentation that I made an immediate appointment with my doctor. He checked out my heart thoroughly and said it was fine. He called my heart experience 'normal tachycardia' and attributed it to nerves. I asked him if he felt a pounding heart when he gave speeches. He shrugged and said no. Lucky him! When this happens, I worry that I am going to have a heart attack. My heart feels like it is going to explode right out of my chest. I sometimes think the audience must see my tie bouncing up and down."

Heart palpitations (the term *palpitation* simply means that the beating of the heart is noticeably felt) have the especially annoying characteristic of getting worse the more one focuses on them. Under the influence of anxiety, the heart beats faster and sometimes with extra, jolt-like beats (extra systoles). These are almost always harmless from a clinical perspective but can nevertheless increase anxiety in performance situations. And with increased anxiety comes a faster and more noticeable heartbeat, much to the consternation of the speaker.

With repeated occurrences of this frightening sensation, many speakers become sensitized to the beating of their heart and feel it more readily than the average person. To gauge the level of their rising anxiety before speaking, these people may take their pulse, often while waiting to present. Any rise in the rate of the pulse sets them to worrying, "It's happening again." Because the pacemakers of the heart slow the pulse rate gradually rather than suddenly, the worried speaker feels powerless to "get my pulse back into a normal range." He or she checks it again and again to see whether the rate is rising or falling. All of this focus on the heart, of course, creates just the upwardly spiraling nervous cycle that the speaker abhors. Panic sets in as the heart beats near its maximum range (some anguished speakers report pulse rates in the 170 range for many minutes at a time).

Some speakers obsessed with heart sensations feel the thud of their rapid pulse in the throat or side of the neck (the feeling of "having one's heart in one's throat," as the expression goes). Others feel the heart pounding in their upper chest. Those who have sensitized themselves to their heartbeat, often over a period of years, may be able to feel pulsing within their fingertips.

The worries that stem from such heart sensations during public speaking spell full employment for cardiologists. Much more often than not, examination of the heart proves clinically negative, with no problems discovered. This reassurance alone is enough for some patients to return to speaking without further concern for their racing pulses. As they learn to ignore their heart at such moments, their heart is less subject to the effects of anxiety and tends to beat at a slower pace and in a less noticeable way. But the reassurance of a thousand doctors is not enough for some speakers, who have convinced themselves against all evidence that their hearts are malfunctioning during speaking occasions and that they are in mortal danger. These are the men and women who unfortunately pass up promotions and opportunities for professional visibility, all because the new jobs involve more public presentations.

Shakiness and Trembling

Washington G., a stock analyst in Boston: "If I have to speak to more than ten people in a room, I get shaky hands, quivering knees, and jittery facial muscles. I don't dare try to pick up a piece of paper when these shakes take over; the audience could see the page fluttering from the back row. And I can't use a pointer against a projection screen. My trembling makes it jump around like a mosquito on a windowpane. What irritates me is that this shaking just won't stop during the presentation, no matter how much I tell myself to calm down. After giving a presentation, I usually find some excuse to leave the room, because my hands are still shaking and my facial muscles are twitching. I don't want to try to talk with someone after the speech if I don't act and feel like myself. And how can you feel like your natural self if you feel your cheek and mouth muscles jerking when you try to smile or talk? I checked with a doctor to see if I had early onset of Parkinson's disease. I didn't. The doctor said it was just speaker's nerves. It may be just speaker's nerves to him, but it is pure hell to me."

Skeletal muscles, particularly those for finer movement (such as finger muscles) and those under stress (such as leg muscles), can contract more quickly than usual under the influence of speaker's nerves. The feeling is not unlike a muscle spasm. Just as quickly, those muscles revert to their relaxed state and then fire again in mini-spasm. The result is shakiness, and the impact on a speaker can be extremely frustrating. Speakers used to controlling hand movements, for example, find in a moment of nerves that fingers vibrate on their own. No exertion of will can make them be still.

Similarly, muscles in the face betray the influence of nerves by sudden jerks. Gone is the speaker's capacity to look cool and collected, especially to those at close range. Smiles look forced, eyes pinch in a grimace, and cheek muscles tighten and release unpredictably. Muscles in the diaphragm can also go into spasm cycles, giving the feeling of "butterflies" in the stomach area.

All this muscular activity (most of it in spite of the speaker's intent) brings with it some unfortunate compensations and adjustments on the speaker's part. To keep fingers from shaking, speakers make the mistake of gripping the sides of the podium or clasping their hands behind their back. While both these maneuvers do hide the shakiness of the hands, they also prevent the speaker from using effective gestures. In an effort to end the irritating sensation of shaky knees, speakers often lock their legs in an "at attention" position or remain behind the podium to hide the telltale flutter of their clothing. These defensive moves make it impossible for the speaker to step freely from one speaking position to another in front of or even amidst the audience.

Nausea and Other Forms of Digestive Tract Upset

Paul L., a supermarket manager with a major Midwest chain: "I can tell almost to the minute when I'm going to start feeling nauseous before a speaking occasion. I'm usually fine an hour or two before my presentation. But when I get to the thirty-minute mark, I feel like a rocket starting its countdown to disaster. I look incessantly at my watch as the dreaded moment gets closer and closer. With about ten minutes to go, I almost always feel a sick wave of nausea pass over me. Friends have told me I turn green. I rarely vomit at these moments. The nauseous feelings build until I can't think of anything except trying to hold down my last meal. I've tried getting some fresh air, nibbling on saltines, and sipping cold water. None of these techniques work for me. When I move weakly to the front of the room to start my speech, it has to be obvious to everyone that I'm not feeling well. The first words out of my mouth are usually mumbled. I have to start over, closer to the microphone, so that people can hear me. Gradually, the nausea starts to subside, and I feel back in control after the first few minutes of my speech. But I would give anything to avoid the awful feelings that come over me each and every time I have to give a major speech. My doctor says it has nothing to do with my stomach; I don't have an ulcer or anything like that. However, I may get an ulcer if I don't stop worrying about my problem with nausea and speaker's nerves."

Nausea and stomach cramping are among the most common symptoms of speaker's nerves—so much so that they have earned a place among the darkly humorous jokes that pertain to speech anxiety:

> In the days of the Roman Colosseum, captured soldiers were regularly thrown to the lions. But one soldier earned a reputation for bravery and managed to save his life by a bold act. When a lion sprang toward him with lunch on its mind, the man whispered something in the lion's ear just at the last moment. The lion cowered, turned a sickly green, and then slunk back into its cage. This happened again and again, with even the empire's fiercest lions turning tail once they had heard what the man whispered. The emperor, curious to understand the man's power over these beasts, promised him his life in exchange for the secret

of how he caused the lions to leave him alone. "It's simple," the soldier told the emperor. "When a lion is about to attack, I just whisper, 'After you've eaten, they're going to ask you to make a short speech.' Works every time."

Jokes aside, few sufferers find any humor in the discomfort they experience from nausea and other forms of digestive upset before speaking. Some speakers scope out the nearest restroom in advance and remain there ("just in case") until a few moments before they have to speak. Others resort to experimentation with all manner of motion-sickness patches, antacids, and acid blockers such as Tagamet and Prilosec to counter their nausea. Few find much lasting comfort in these attempts.

The full range of digestive upsets can involve stomach cramping, the frequent need to urinate, and diarrhea. Speakers make themselves even more nervous at the prospect of finding themselves in midspeech and having to excuse themselves to sprint to the restroom. This anxiety only adds fuel to the churning fire of internal discomfort.

Excessive Perspiration

Peggy U., a civic leader in Chicago: "I am not the kind of person who sweats profusely, even on the tennis court. But when I get up to give a presentation, my perspiration glands go into overdrive. I feel my forehead break out in beads of moisture, which on the worst occasions have actually plinked off my nose during the speech. Dark perspiration circles start to appear under my arms on the suit or blouse I'm wearing. My hands are literally wet with sweat, and I'm terribly embarrassed before or after my speech to shake hands with anyone. The first time this perspiration problem happened, I assumed the room was unusually warm. But since that time, it has happened again and again, even in rooms where I purposely turned down the air-conditioning to near-arctic conditions to see if that could stop my out-of-control perspiration. No luck. There's no other time in my life where this sweat problem occurs. Therefore, my doctor doesn't want to treat it medically. It's just speaker's nerves, she says. Easy for her to say. She doesn't have my dry-cleaning bill."

In the movie *Broadcast News*, Albert Brooks plays a supporting role to the lead anchorman character, played by William Hurt. At one point, Brooks has the opportunity to step in for Hurt on the nationwide evening news. Intellectually, Brooks is clearly Hurt's superior and, as such, has every confidence that he, Brooks, will succeed as a stand-in anchor. But Brooks did not foresee a violent attack of speaker's nerves in the form of pints, quarts, and then gallons of perspiration pouring from his face, neck, and sopped blazer. He gutted his way through the half-hour broadcast and slunk away looking like a drowned rat.

We have all felt the hot flush of sudden emotion and the moist brow that accompanies it. Speaker's nerves amplifies this response to the point that perspiration becomes not a response to emotion but its own stimulus to emotion, particularly feelings of embarrassment and self-consciousness. We find ourselves in a closed loop: we sweat because we are nervous, and then we become more nervous because we sweat.

Speakers routinely overestimate the audience's ability—or its interest, for that matter—to actually see the perspiration that speakers worry so much about. The sensation of having a drop or two of sweat slide down one's cheek is so apparent to the speaker that he or she assumes the audience also sees the drops and feels them vicariously. Not so. Audiences usually are unaware of the speaker's facial perspiration. When audience members in the first rows do notice perspiration, they tend to chalk it up to effort and energy on the part of the speaker: "You put a lot of enthusiasm into that speech. It showed!"

Mental Lapses Under Stress

Rachel O., a human resources specialist in New England: "No matter how many times I practice my speech, I never know when I'm going to go blank and look like a deer in the headlights to the audience. It's a weird feeling, like not being able to remember the name of someone you've known for years. I've resorted to writing out every last word of what I want to say, but this doesn't guarantee that I won't go blank. The last time I spoke at a company convention, I got through the first three paragraphs of my speech and was looking out at the audience when, wham, my mind just went to zero. I looked down at my speech manuscript and had to quickly reread my opening paragraphs to figure out where I was supposed to be. Needless to say, it was embarrassing. I looked unprepared to my bosses."

Some speakers plagued by a tendency to go blank under the stress of speaker's nerves find that any unexpected sight or noise—an odd hat in the audience or the crash of a plate dropped by a waiter—is enough to blitz their concentration and send them into a moment or two of mental whiteout. Speakers report, "I just felt frozen," and, "I couldn't remember what I was saying before or what I wanted to say next." In these moments, the clutch of panic sets in almost immediately, delaying even further the speaker's effort to find his or her place to continue.

Although there are medical conditions such as catalepsis and epilepsy that cause similar onsets of blankness, the garden-variety interruption described here is not an illness or a physical defect. Some speakers find they are in danger of going blank only in the first minute or two of their speech, when nerves are at their zenith. Others have experienced moments of blankness later in their presentation, when they begin to relax and loosen their mental grip and concentration on their topic. For all, the unpredictability of the going-blank experience is its most worrisome aspect.

Even in their efforts to minimize these occurrences, speakers find themselves in a dilemma. If they overplan their presentation, with detailed notes or actual manuscript for everything they want to say, the stress of the preparation itself can make an involuntary mental time-out more likely. But if they relax and trust their ability to wing it with the audience, they also may find themselves plunging rather than flying high as a presenter.

James Baker, former secretary of state, experienced such a moment of blankness in an address to the National Press Club. He began one portion of his speech by referring to three reasons why the president had taken a controversial action. After describing the first two reasons, Baker hit an obvious blank, looked down at his notes without luck, and then sheepishly looked to his aides offstage. "What was that third reason?" he chuckled. They rescued him, and he continued on with a highly successful presentation.

In a movie version of the same phenomenon, Kevin Kline in *A Fish Called Wanda* plays a garrulous character who is forever asking, "What was that middle part?" These kinds of lapses have nothing to do with forgetfulness, mental acuity, or intelligence. They have been likened with some truth to overload breakers on electrical circuits. Under the stress of audience expectations and internal motivation to do well, the speaker's mind can "flip out" for a moment and simply refuse to move forward with the program.

Jitteriness, Darting Eyes, Pacing, and Repetitive Gestures

Owen T., owner of a car dealership in Arizona: "I'm a mess when I speak; that's all I can say. My eyes drift up to the ceiling or down at the carpet or flit around the faces in the audience as if I were on some drug trip. I can't just look at people and talk to them calmly as if they were in my own living room. I practically wear a path in my pacing back and forth in front of the room. The audience looks like it's watching a tennis match when I'm speaking. And whatever gesture I start using at the beginning of my speech is the one I seem to use over and over through the rest of the speech, whether it's shaking one finger at the audience or rubbing my hands together or making a fist to punctuate each one of my points. All the time, I feel jittery, as if I had drunk a half-dozen cups of coffee in a row. My craziness is obvious to the audience. I see them looking at one another with raised eyebrows and questioning looks when I speak. They obviously think I'm an oddball. I doubt that they are able to listen to what I'm saying. They can't help but be preoccupied with all my frenetic and nervous antics—all unintended, I assure you!"

"The jitters" is a catchall category for a wide range of afflictions reported by those who suffer from speaker's nerves. High anxiety, in Mel Brooks's term, can cause the following irritating surprises for speakers:

- Cracking voice
- Unnatural pitch (the "monotone" drone)
- Inappropriate volume (speaking too softly or too loudly)

- Mistakes in pace and pauses (speaking too quickly and without breaks)
- Inattention to surrounding details (a slide that didn't change as planned or an ignored question from the audience)

The sustained experience of jitters through a prolonged speech can be exhausting. Some speakers take days to recover emotionally from the stress of a speech. They claim to lose pounds through perspiration from the giving of the speech and from their inability to eat for days before the presentation. Tired to the core, they resolve to avoid public speaking whenever possible.

Embarrassment, Self-Consciousness, and Awkwardness

Susan D., restaurant owner in San Francisco: "My experience of speaker's nerves is more mental than physical. I have no trouble relating to people in general; in my restaurant, in fact, I enjoy going around to tables of regulars and total strangers to strike up conversation. But last year I had to speak at a restaurant convention in front of five hundred people. As I stepped behind the podium to speak, I felt waves of self-accusation pouring over me: you've chosen the wrong outfit, your makeup is wrong for the stage lights, your facial expressions look goofy and insincere, your voice sounds like Minnie Mouse, and so forth. Rationally, I knew these things to be untrue. My fears and self-doubts were irrational but extremely powerful. I was glad to survive the speaking occasion and promised myself, 'Never again!'"

Embarrassment, self-consciousness, and awkwardness usually do not stem from any one thing the speaker did (such as spilling the glass of water on the podium). These feelings arise, entirely uninvited, from feelings of isolation and ostracism in the presence of the audience. The phenomenon has been called the "new kid at school" syndrome. Until we make acquaintances and friends in a new social environment, we often can't help being hyperaware of what we're wearing, what we're saying, how we're looking at others, where we're sitting at lunch, and so forth. When these strong inner concerns and messages flood the mind of a speaker, he or she understandably has trouble focusing on the presentation at hand.

Obsessed with self-conscious thoughts, the speaker may tend to just read the speech in an effort to "get through it" as quickly as possible. If self-consciousness causes the speaker to bobble his or her words or skip an important sentence, those glitches only add to the inner noise of accusations and feelings of failure.

Importantly, feelings of embarrassment, self-consciousness, and awkwardness can occur even when the speaker is delivering a presentation to people he or she knows quite well. The genesis of such feelings lies not in the actual relationship between the speaker and the audience but instead in what the speaker *believes* (consciously or subconsciously) about the audience.

Simultaneous and Sequential Experiences of Speaker's Nerves

As mentioned at the outset of this chapter, the symptoms identified individually in this chapter rarely appear by themselves in the absence of any other symptoms. Those who suffer from speaker's nerves do tend to name one particular symptom that bothers them most of all—"my sweaty palms," for example, or "my heart"—and this tendency can give the impression that no other symptoms were involved in the experience. But in calmer moments, when these people reflect on what they experienced, they inevitably identify secondary feelings and sensations that either occurred at the same time as the onset of speaker's nerves or came on sequentially, one by one.

Here are three typical "clusters" of feelings, in the descriptions of sufferers themselves.

The Heart–Breathing–Faintness Syndrome

A midlevel manager giving her first major company presentation: "I first felt that I couldn't catch my breath. That scared me and made my heart begin to race. When I felt my pulse climbing above 100, I started to hyperventilate, which made me feel like I was going to faint. I had to sit down and put my head lower than my knees to keep from passing out."

When the body perceives itself to be in crisis (even an imagined crisis), blood flow is redirected to major organs such as the heart. A temporary but frightening feeling of lightheadedness can occur as blood pressure changes. A clutch of panic can ensue, further amplifying feelings of tachycardia (rapid heartbeat) and breathlessness.

The Skin–Perspiration–Temperature Syndrome

A small-business owner speaking for the first time to his Rotary Club: "I could feel my neck getting warm as I rose to speak, and I knew that those hideous red blotches were probably starting to appear. I thought everyone was staring at them and not hearing a word I was saying. The more I worried about the blotches, the more I felt perspiration breaking out on my forehead and then, in a cold and clammy way, across my entire body. My hands were sweaty, and the room suddenly seemed frigid. I shivered even though I was covered in perspiration."

With rising blood pressure comes a rosier complexion—and, for some people, noticeable blotching. These symptoms are usually associated with embarrassment ("she blushed a crimson red"). When a speaker doubles, as it were, the natural reddening that comes with rising blood pressure with an additional adrenaline surge due to embarrassment over blotching, the result can be a flood of panic responses, often felt as uncontrollable perspiration across the entire body. Evaporation then brings feelings of chilliness, as body temperature adjusts to the sudden bath of moisture.

The Trembling–Rigid Posture Syndrome

A new professor on the first day of class: "I went to place my page of notes on the podium and realized that the paper was shaking like a leaf. My hands were visibly trembling. I didn't know how I would gesture without embarrassing myself, so I clamped my hands onto the edges of the podium and held on for dear life. About that time, my knees and upper leg muscles started to shake. I moved closer to the podium to hide my lower body as much as possible. I tried to keep my knees and legs from shaking by tightening my muscles. In this frozen position, I gave my lecture as quickly as I could and somehow got back to my office alive."

The increased adrenaline that comes with speech anxiety dramatically affects muscle synapses (the firing of nerves that control muscle response). In a true life-or-death situation, such nervous edginess of the muscles makes for faster, stronger response to danger. But in a public speaking situation, muscles are only at the ready in terms of their nervous stimulation and don't expend their energy in running away or striking back. The result is commonly felt as "the shakes." In an effort to control this sensation, some speakers try to tense major muscles in their legs, arms, torso, and neck. These individuals strive to overcome shakiness by holding themselves in a rigid (and quite uncomfortable) posture. The strategy backfires by making natural gestures, movement, and facial expression impossible.

Speaker's Nerves Across Differences in Age, Gender, and Profession

The experience of speaker's nerves, or performance anxiety in general, is no respecter of age. Toastmasters International, the popular speakers' organization, has given millions of men and women of all age groups the chance to practice public speaking in front of other adults. In these venues, across cultures and regions, speaker's nerves plague twenty-year-olds in the same way and to the same degree that seventy-year-olds are afflicted. Men and women show no significant variation by gender in the frequency or severity of speaker's nerves. We are all in this together.

Nor does one's profession or level of education appear to influence whether one will feel the pinch or smack of speaker's nerves. A banker with an MBA is as likely to experience speaker's nerves as a farmer who has not completed high school. Ironically, if anything, speaker's nerves can be observed more often in highly motivated, success-oriented people (such as students with high GPAs) than in more relaxed, middle-of-the-pack individuals.

Of all fear-related emotional and physical sensations, speaker's nerves appears to be the great leveler among human beings. It is regularly named, in surveys in the *New York Times* and elsewhere, as the number one fear of people generally, surpassing by a significant margin the fear of spiders, snakes, and even death.

Although speaker's nerves is the most common human fear, it remains the least understood for the countless millions who experience it. When asked, "What are you afraid of?" many sufferers respond, "I don't know," "It's nothing and it's everything," and "I'm just being silly." Others attribute their fear to personal characteristics: "I'm too self-conscious"; "I'm afraid I will fail"; and "I worry about looking and sounding like a fool." Still others blame the circumstances or audience: "I didn't have time to prepare"; "I was nervous because the audience seemed bored"; and "No one was listening because dessert was still being served."

Degrees of Severity in Speaker's Nerves

What matters most in your experience of speaker's nerves is not the objective measurement of symptoms (for example, the volume of perspiration, the actual rate of your heartbeat, or the pace of your breathing) but instead your subjective impression of and response to those symptoms. A slight blushing across the cheeks may send one speaker into nervous worries, while another speaker doesn't think twice about huge blotches of red spreading across his neck (but perhaps reacts in panic to a fast heartbeat).

In *Tristram Shandy*, author Laurence Sterne shrewdly observed, "Each man rides his own hobby-horse." That is, each of us selects, often subconsciously, the objects or stimuli to which we give our primary attention—or our fear, in the case of speaker's nerves. These stimuli may seem absurd to others. "Why are you worried about a fast heartbeat?" a coworker may say. "Your heart beats that fast every time we play tennis." Or, "So what if you perspire when you speak? I think sweat is natural." But the fact that others don't concur with the reasonableness of our fears doesn't keep us from obsessing about certain symptoms. Irrational or not, these symptoms are "ours." And other people, we realize, probably have their own stimuli to nervousness that no doubt seem odd and irrational to us. The point is that, whether sensible or not, we have selected a highly personal hobby-horse to ride in our experience of speaker's nerves. The question we will address in Chapter 4 is how to tame that animal and make the ride more enjoyable for ourselves and others.

Factors Involved in Speaker's Nerves

Confrontations with speaker's nerves do not necessarily happen the first time a person makes a presentation. Students who had "no sweat" giving speeches throughout high school sometimes run into the apparent brick wall of nerves in their first college presentation. Adults who speak often and freely in their occupations can still experience speaker's nerves when they rise at a town council meeting to protest a zoning change or other matter. Many variables affect when and how a person confronts speaker's nerves:

- **Change in the size and composition of the audience.** Often the demographics of an audience can be a stimulus to nervousness for speakers. Faculty members who are used to talking to young adults by the hour may experience the clutch of terror when asked to make a presentation before the dean's advisory board or even their fellow faculty members. A businessperson who regularly gives briefings to the eighteen members of her work group can freeze up with nerves when assigned the task of speaking to five hundred people at a company convention.

- **Stakes involved in the situation.** Some presentations, from a career or status point of view, are more crucial than others. If the speaker feels it's essential to "do or die" in giving a fabulous presentation, speaker's nerves more likely will come into play. By contrast, a speech given in a circumstance where nothing is to be gained or lost holds much less potential for a bout with nerves. Politicians typically feel more stress, often to the point of speaker's nerves, in their kickoff campaign speech compared with the relaxation they feel in their thank-you speech to campaign workers after the election.

- **Speaker's general health and state of restedness.** When a businessperson, still jet-lagged, jumps off a plane from Tokyo and rushes by cab across town to give a major presentation, he or she is more likely to experience speaker's nerves than the colleague who slept well the night before the speech. A person coming off the flu or other short-term illness can be vulnerable to nervous symptoms and stress in a way that the same person isn't during periods of robust health.

- **Location.** Nineteenth-century poets, including Wordsworth and Keats, referred often to the "spirit of the spot," as if certain locations brought with them a contagion of particular thoughts and feelings. Some speaking locations can prove reassuring to speakers—the "good old boardroom," for example, or "my favorite restaurant"—while other locations, however grand, can be intimidating. Giving a speech in the familiar surroundings of one's corporate headquarters can feel quite different from giving the same speech in a ballroom at the Ritz. The latter venue, for many speakers, carries with it associations of superb performance, excellent quality, and past heritage, all of which can bring on speaker's nerves for the speaker who worries, "What am I doing here?"

- **Time of day.** Without invoking the dubious notion of circadian rhythms, we can at least observe that some of us are "morning people," while others aren't. Some hit their stride in the later hours of the evening, while others are ready for bed. If asked to make a presentation at a time when you're not at your best, there's an increased chance that you will be prone to speaker's nerves.

- **Speaker's sense of emotional well-being.** The effort and excitement involved in giving a presentation can be the straw that broke the camel's back if loaded upon an already burdened emotional life. It is hardly surprising that an individual going through a divorce or recovering from the death of a loved one may be close to nervous exhaustion and vulnerable to speaker's nerves.

- **Experiences in speaking situations.** Speaker's nerves can increase or decrease depending on how the speaker remembers and interprets prior speaking experiences. For example, a manager who has given three business talks over a period of months to highly critical customer audiences may easily develop a loathing for such speeches—and act out that loathing, subconsciously, with an attack of speaker's nerves. In contrast, a speaker who has had progressively more and more favorable receptions from audiences often (but not always) feels the grip of speaker's nerves loosen, replaced by the thrill of an energized, enthusiastic delivery. The "but not always" qualifier is inserted just to remind us that growing praise can also increase the pressure on some speakers, who experience speaker's nerves precisely because so much is expected of them. In other words, they worry about whether they can live up to their growing reputations.

Episodic and Unpredictable Speaker's Nerves

Perhaps most distressing of all for many speakers are bouts with speech anxiety that seem to follow no pattern or rationale. Cheryl R., a Seattle real estate broker, tells of her lifelong battle against sporadic occurrences of speaker's nerves: "It started in sixth grade. I was just entering puberty, a bit overweight, and the target of cruel teasing by several kids in the class. Over my protestations, the teacher forced me to give a ten-minute speech to the class on whales. I could see and hear the sniggers of my classmates as I tried to talk. I felt simultaneously petrified and mortified. After a minute or two of speaking, I just ended up looking down at my script and reading it word for word as fast as I could. I still remember it as the worst moment of my life.

"Since then, I've given many presentations in college, professional seminars, and real estate meetings and conventions. Usually these go quite well, and I receive applause and compliments. But every once in a while—I would say 10 percent of the time—I feel my sixth-grade dread of public speaking well up within me, usually just before I stand up to speak. It's crazy. I don't know when it will strike or why. It doesn't seem to be associated with large audiences or small groups, big halls or small rooms. The unpredictability of these feelings is what drives me nuts. I don't know when they will strike. I'm constantly asking myself before a presentation, 'Is it going to happen this time? And how will I cope if it does?'"

Speaker's nerves that we usually hold in check sometimes, without warning, can break through the fragile threshold of our control. Why one time and not another? The answer to that riddle can be as complex as our physical and psychological lives. Physical factors such as caffeine from a couple of extra cups of coffee, alcohol from a lunchtime cocktail, or an abundance of sugar from a rich dessert can sometimes play a role in putting us "over the edge" into bouts with speaker's nerves. Hormone levels can push unwelcome emotions our way, as is often the case for women in menopause or for men facing testosterone changes. Sleep deprivation can influence moods and nervousness in profound and unexpected ways, as can stress from relationship or financial problems.

When speaker's nerves strike out of the blue, it's advisable to seek sources of physical or emotional stress that may explain them and, once resolved, can relieve them. But don't be surprised if the search for specific causes turns out to be a prolonged and frustrating pursuit. Many sufferers from sporadic attacks of speaker's nerves find that just when they believe they have located the underlying culprit ("It's speaking right after I've eaten!"), up pops an attack under completely different circumstances, upsetting the theory and sending them back into search mode.

Summing Up

The symptoms of speaker's nerves can be described in practical, down-to-earth ways and also in the language of human physiology. The former accords with what we feel when we are in the grip of speaker's nerves. The latter is useful as reassuring background information for what, in fact, is going on inside our bodies during bouts with speaker's nerves. Although speakers tend to focus on one symptom as predominant over others, symptoms tend to cluster (heart–breathing–faintness, skin–perspiration–temperature, trembling–rigid posture). Symptoms can rise or fall in severity, depending on many factors as interpreted by the speaker, including size and composition of audience, stakes involved in the presentation, the speaker's general health, the location, the time of day, the speaker's emotional well-being, and the speaker's experiences in presenting.

2

Understanding Speaker's Nerves
from the Body's Perspective

"I'M SO MAD at myself," an executive at a major clothing retailer told me. "I prepared thoroughly for my speech at the company's national sales meeting. I even videotaped one of my practice sessions to make sure I looked and sounded as professional as possible. But when the moment came to give the speech, my body let me down! My heart raced, I was bathed in perspiration, and I could hardly get through the speech without passing out. I had this speech absolutely wired in my mind. I didn't think my body would mess things up."

Speaker's nerves, as described in detail in Chapter 1, are felt in large part as bodily, physical sensations. When such feelings disrupt a speaker's confidence and professionalism in speaking, it's natural to blame the apparent source of the symptom—that is, the heart, the stomach, the body's perspiration system, and so forth. It's common for nervous speakers to rush to their physicians in an effort to discover "what's wrong with my body," even though the real cause of their symptoms often lies in the rational mind and emotions.

In this chapter, we give the body a chance to explain, as it were, what it thinks it is doing during an attack of speaker's nerves. Although the body doesn't literally speak, we can nevertheless look within ourselves as individuals and as a species to discover a physical rationale for nervous symptoms. By listening to our bodies (as New Age as that phrase may inadvertently sound), we can understand that our physical responses to stress and fright are not random, accidental, or senseless. The body has definite goals in mind when it sets the heart racing, causes the palms to sweat, and produces all the other symptoms of speaker's nerves. Far from letting us down, our bodies are under the impression that they are acting in our best interests through such physical sensations. The remainder of this chapter explores these responses in a general way, and Chapter 7 provides clinical and scientific details of what the body experiences under the influence of speaker's nerves, for readers who desire a more physiological explanation.

The Physical Evolution of Speaker's Nerves

The story of the human body's rationale for nervous symptoms goes back long before your childhood and even your birth. (This insight alone can be a relief to nervous sufferers who may have blamed teachers, parents, and an ugly clown for symptoms of speaker's nerves carried into adulthood.) We can reach back at least 250,000 years in human evolution to a crucial question for our ancient ancestors: how should the central nervous system best be "wired" for the sake of survival? No committee sat around to make this decision, of course; human evolution took its course according to what worked and didn't work.

What did not work in evolutionary terms—spectacularly so—was precisely what most of us want with regard to speaker's nerves: a calm, settled feeling that isn't worried or disturbed by what's going on around us. That feeling in human development (the first "endorphin high"?), for all its emotional warmth and cuddliness, didn't work out particularly well when lions, tigers, and bears (all in their prehistoric form, of course) were circling outside the cave. The evolutionary survival mechanism that did save our ancestors' bacon was the body's ability to go on full alert, however uncomfortable that might have been: eyes and ears hyperalert to signs and sounds of danger, heart and lungs revving up to prepare for battle or escape, perspiration prickling out to cool the head for decision making and the body for maximum exertion. Irritating symptoms? No doubt— unless we compare them to the sensation of being eaten by a saber-toothed tiger.

The net result of the development of neural pathways in the earliest humans, and their ancestors before them, is this: sensory messages sent at lightning speed from the eyes, ears, skin, and other stimuli receptors are routed first to a powerful, automatic "triage" center in the oldest part of our brain, the amygdala. Here a near-instant assessment is made. Are these sensory messages signaling something urgent that threatens the individual's survival?

If so, the amygdala (without asking permission, as it were, from the rational processes in the cerebral cortex, the more modern part of the brain in evolutionary terms) sends a powerful electrochemical alarm in a split second through the nerve and hormone systems to major organs in the body. "Get ready to fight or flee," the amygdala in effect says (obviously not in words) to these organs. "You have to be ready to save your life!" At a conscious level, you won't have much luck arguing with your amygdala. First, it acts too quickly for you to debate its decisions. Second, it plays a key role in keeping your heart beating and your breathing regulated, neither of which you would want under your minute-by-minute conscious control. Finally, major nerve pathways connect to the amygdala before they are routed on to higher levels of cognition. The amygdala literally has first chance at processing and interpreting signals from your nerve endings.

The great majority of physical symptoms associated with speaker's nerves can be accounted for (though not dismissed) by understanding what the amygdala and its automatic alarm system is trying to achieve. You have read newspaper and television reports of some of the dramatic aspects of the fight-or-flight response kicked off by the amygdala: individuals suddenly strong enough to push automobiles off themselves or others and other seemingly Herculean feats. Less publicized but much more common are the alarms set off by the amygdala during times of sudden stress or fear.

Ten Fight-or-Flight Messages to the Parts of the Body

Let's consider ten fight-or-flight strategies set in motion by the amygdala, as a way of understanding more deeply what we're feeling during bouts with speaker's nerves. To grasp the picture as our prehistoric brain perceives it, imagine yourself 250,000 years ago, headed back to your cave after a successful day of hunting and gathering. Suddenly you spot a huge saber-toothed tiger. Worse, it spots you.

Message to the Heart

When the amygdala interprets a wave of nervous stimuli as a threat, it responds by increasing the heart rate and raising the blood pressure. In an actual battle or sprint for your life, this increased circulation would give you the physical energy to fight the beast or, preferably, run away. Your increased heart rate provides maximum energy to your major muscles—legs, arms, and torso. "But," you may rightly object, "a PTA meeting is hardly a saber-toothed tiger. Why is my amygdala driving me crazy with fight-or-flight alarms when I'm not physically in danger?"

In fact, the amygdala does not know you are not in physical danger. It receives a wave of nervous stimuli (your fear of getting up to speak at the PTA meeting) that, in electrochemical form, are exactly like the signals received some 250,000 years ago in the eye of the tiger. As an emergency, quick-reaction center, the amygdala is not wired to send conscious messages: "Are you sure you're not threatened? Do you want to check to make sure?" This kind of double-checking could have cost *Homo sapiens* its very existence at an earlier evolutionary period. When the tiger pounces, there's no time for second-guessing. Of course, had the amygdala not done its job at that time, our problems with speaker's nerves would have been resolved. We wouldn't be here to get nervous.

Message to the Lungs

Just as the heart rate is increased to near maximum, so our breathing speeds up under perceived threat. This change is aimed at bringing in as much oxygen as possible when we inhale and casting off exhaled carbon dioxide, the exhaust of our metabolism. Some people experience this increased breathing rate as fast, shallow panting (the kind of sensation you may have felt after slamming on your brakes in a near-miss auto situation); others experience deep, chest-filling breathing of the sort practiced by competitive swimmers and runners before the starting gun fires. In both cases, the amygdala has signaled the breathing apparatus to do its part in preparation for fight or flight.

As described in dozens of yoga books, an increased rate or depth of breathing can create an energetic feeling. But that energy, in a fight-or-flight scenario, has to "go somewhere"—that is, be spent in muscular activity. Otherwise, we end up in the physical limbo of hyperventilation. Contrary to urban myth, hyperventilation is not caused by the overabundance of oxygen in the blood. Instead, the cause is an imbalance in the blood gases of carbon dioxide, which we are exhaling too quickly. This tendency to blow off carbon dioxide too quickly afflicts nervous speakers who feel they have to rush through their presentation and get away from the dreaded podium as quickly as possible. They end up with the classic symptoms of hyperventilation: lightheadedness, tingly fingers and cheeks, a general feeling of suffocation ("can't get enough air"), and a darkening of peripheral vision. In an extreme state of hyperventilation, some speakers pass out (Winston Churchill's experience in his first speech to Parliament), at which point breathing generally returns to normal, the hyperventilation subsides, and the person awakes with a "what happened?" look.

Message to the Salivary System

Back at the ranch, the saber-toothed tiger is still there, crouching in preparation for an entree you would prefer not to serve. Your mouth goes dry, as does your throat—accounting for the cracking or squeaking voice heard from a nervous speaker, whose vocal cords are tightened by nervous stress and dried by lack of saliva. The amygdala has temporarily shut down the saliva system in order, once again, to save you from becoming one with the tiger, as Zen masters say. If you are indeed going to gulp in maximum amounts of air in your fight-or-flight struggle, it simply will not do to have you choke on your own saliva.

The feeling of a dry mouth and throat is particularly upsetting to some speakers, who find that they stumble over words and phrases — in short, experience a tangled tongue. From the point of view of the amygdala, your ability to pronounce words clearly during a time of primal attack from the tiger is hardly a priority. The amygdala, with some evolutionary wisdom, makes the judgment call that the tiger will not be dissuaded from its menu selection based on anything you say. A few verbal stumbles, from this perspective, are a small price indeed for the fight-or-flight benefit of having unrestricted airways for maximum breathing capacity.

Message to the Hands and Feet

With the onset of a threat, real or imagined, the amygdala quickly prioritizes where energy-sustaining blood should be centralized in the body. Major blood vessels surrounding the heart and lungs expand in keeping with rising blood pressure. Minor blood vessels, such as those extending to the fingers and toes, are signaled by the primal brain to squeeze almost shut. The result is cold hands and feet, sometimes almost to the point of numbness. In a fight-or-flight situation, manual dexterity or your ability to play "Chopsticks" with your toes is a luxury the body cannot afford. All its resources must be devoted to the major organs and muscles that will be primarily responsible for saving your life. At most, the hand will only have to form into a fist for fighting (a deeply instinctual reflex position you can observe in many nervous speakers, whose knuckles are white from a tight-fisted grip on the podium).

No wonder so many speakers complain of difficulty in making natural, graceful gestures when they try to speak under the influence of nerves. Conscious of the fact that their hands are not helping their presentation, these speakers attempt to warm them in several unsatisfactory ways:

- Sticking their hands in the pockets of their pants or jacket
- Clasping their hands rigidly behind their back (the "parade rest" position) or just as self-consciously in front (the "fig leaf" position)
- Rubbing their hands together, almost as if trying to ignite a fire

- Knitting their fingers in a "here's the church, here's the steeple" position or, just as annoying over the course of a presentation, in a praying position
- Massaging their fingers and knuckles, stopping along the way to twist at a ring or bracelet
- Shifting their weight from one numb foot to the other or shuffling uneasily in an effort to increase circulation

In all these ways, speakers try to override or at least hide the amygdala's logical strategy to choose life (through blood supply to major organs and muscles) over comfort to the hands and feet.

Message to the Perspiration System

Car radiators are stressed, sometimes to the breaking point, by high engine temperatures occasioned by driving up steep hills and carrying heavy loads. The human radiation system, perspiration, has a similar task of carrying away heat from increased muscular activity and metabolism, so that our narrow temperature range of 97 to 101 degrees or so can be maintained in stress situations. If our body temperature falls out of that range, we quickly find ourselves overcome by weakness and lethargy, unable to fight the tiger or run away. The switch for turning this invaluable system on and off, predictably, is located in the amygdala. Within less than a second of perceiving a threat, our body can break out all over in perspiration intended to cool us for a potential epic struggle.

That physical rationale may not be of much comfort to the speaker whose perspiration is literally plinking off his or her nose while everyone else in the room seems quite comfortable. Not a few speakers have opted to wear more clothing (a suit jacket or blazer, for example) in an effort to hide perspiration spots spreading beneath the arms of their shirt or blouse. Of course, this "cover it" approach holds in the body's heat, stimulating even more perspiration. The cold hands mentioned earlier become truly frigid and clammy when bathed in perspiration. Unused to wet hands on a cool day, speakers clasp and unclasp them, rub them against the top of the podium, or try to dry them inconspicuously inside their pockets. One television commentator notes that baseball players, notoriously nervous in front of the microphone, usually wear their baseball glove during the interview and bury their throwing hand into the glove in the form of a tight fist.

Perspiration on the face is particularly bothersome to many speakers. They feel drops of sweat beading up on their forehead but are conflicted about whether to wipe off their brow (thus calling attention to the perspiration but increasing their comfort) or simply letting drops turn into rivulets coursing down their cheeks. Because the speaker feels the perspiration intensely, he or she assumes that the audience can see it as well. In fact, audiences are rarely aware of a speaker's damp forehead or moist neck unless the speaker calls attention to it by constantly dabbing at his or her forehead or pulling at his or her collar.

The hot lights or "sun guns" used by media in interview situations certainly don't help a speaker already prone to excessive perspiration. Many female executives appearing for the first time on camera become upset by waves of perspiration that undo their makeup. Male executives, less vulnerable to the makeup problem, also experience difficulty under the hot lights. Men tend to think that visible facial perspiration in close camera shots makes them look weak, guilty, or dissembling.

Message to the Digestive System

The saber-toothed tiger's digestive system is roaring full tilt in preparation for a wonderful meal (you) and then a long nap. Your amygdala, by contrast, is signaling just the opposite to your stomach, intestines, bladder, and bowels. "Don't even think about eating!" the amygdala tells these organs. "In fact, if you just ate, do whatever is necessary to lighten your load." The amygdala wisely wants all body resources, including the blood supply, ready to serve the emergency needs of fight or flight. If a caveman ate a wildebeest sandwich just before spotting the saber-toothed tiger, the amygdala would send powerful waves of nausea through his body in an effort to put off digestion, shall we say, for a better time. Diarrhea and incontinence, similarly, are common experiences in response to the amygdala's urgent call for a light, mean, and lean fighting machine.

The term *butterflies* is certainly a polite, even poetic, way to describe what many nervous speakers experience before, during, and sometimes after their presentations. When stomach muscles twist and turn, few speakers think of butterflies. The nausea that often accompanies such digestive acrobatics keeps some speakers in the wings (or in the restroom) until just before they have to step forward to speak. At luncheon occasions, relatively few speakers truly enjoy a good meal before rising to speak. The natural interference of signals from the amygdala makes chicken taste like, well, chicken and the rest of the meal like mush. Interestingly, some nervous speakers report a heightening of taste sensations before a speaking occasion, so that coffee or iced tea that would have been enjoyable at an earlier time now tastes bitter and sour. The amygdala doesn't pull punches when it wants to tell the entire digestive system, from taste buds to tummy, to "just say no" in one way or another to food that could interfere with the fight-or-flight response.

Message to the Eyes

Face-to-face with the saber-toothed tiger, our caveman experiences the takeover of his eye muscles by the amygdala. Highly adrenalized, his eyes flit wildly in all directions, no doubt in a fear-born response to evaluate his immediate environment for possible escape routes. These are the "rabbit eyes" familiar to nervous speakers and their audiences. The speaker can't seem to hold any one person in focus for more than a split second, but instead lets his or her eyes wander frantically and jerkily across the faces of the audience. An audience member lucky enough to catch a nanosecond of eye contact from the speaker is quickly discouraged from any real rapport as the speaker abruptly twitches his or her eyes elsewhere.

Speakers (or cavepersons) who manage to resist rabbit eyes may still fall into the instinctual eye patterns of looking heavenward or at their feet under the influence of threat, whether from a tiger or an audience. We have all observed speakers who stare at the ceiling for most of their presentation, as if fascinated by the pipes, tiles, or water stains there. Or the carpet can claim a speaker's obsessive focus, with his or her eyes peeking up only once in a while to see if the audience (or tiger) is still there. These upward or downward eye patterns stem from old evolutionary defenses: "If I pretend I don't see the tiger, perhaps the tiger won't see me." Jane Goodall, in her work with dominant male gorillas, made it a practice to avert her gaze as a way of avoiding hostile encounters.

If we practiced these odd eye patterns in daily life, we would quickly lose any semblance of a social life. You could not, for example, go to a friend's house for dinner and then look at the ceiling or floor for the entire evening. You could not talk lovingly to your significant other while your eyes were flitting frenetically about, like those of an amphetamine addict. In short, what you signal with your eyes matters powerfully for rapport with other people. The eye patterns stimulated by primal amygdala influence have to be countermanded by your conscious control over how your eyes appear to others. Probably more than any other nonverbal signal, your eyes tell your listeners volumes about your self-confidence, your attitude toward them, and your willingness to receive the signals they are simultaneously sending you with their eyes and faces.

Message to the Cheeks and Neck

As blood pressure and heartbeat rise in response to the commands of the amygdala, a speaker's cheeks, neck, and upper chest can sometimes break out into florets of blush that rival Gainesborough's *Pink Lady*. This florid display, mortifying to some speakers and not worth thinking about for others, may be one of the oldest and most primitive responses to perceived threat. The amygdala's effort, again, is to do whatever it can to promote survival. Coloration of the cheeks, neck, and upper chest can be a signal, as it is in many primates and other animals, that one's courage is screwed to the sticking point—"Game on, tiger!" Native tribes throughout the world practice a similar strategy in facial displays of war paint. Even women's makeup, especially in its more overt use, can be interpreted as a power play, as many conquered men will attest, in the battle of the sexes.

Speakers, unfortunately, do not usually regard their blotches as signs of courage and commitment to the struggle at hand. They see these marks as red badges of cowardice, bodily telltales that they are roiling within and only faking the outward confidence communicated by their words. One speaker called her red blotches her "Benedict Arnolds"—traitors that betrayed her anxieties to the audience.

Audiences, in contrast, tend to be less judgmental if they observe reddening on the speaker's face or neck (and audiences often do not bother to look so closely). Listeners by and large do not assume that the speaker is falling apart from inner angst or melting with embarrassment and lack of confidence just because bright red spots appear on his or her cheeks. "Your cheeks turned really red," one listener said to a friend who had just completed a personally harrowing presentation. "Oh God," the friend said. "Was it really that obvious?" She was surprised when the listener explained, "It was nothing. I just noticed your cheeks got red. That's all."

Message to the Brain

It may seem strange that the amygdala, as part of the brain, can influence other parts of the brain. But indeed it does, as many speakers can describe: "I went blank"; "I couldn't remember my boss's name"; "I had my speech completely memorized, but it just evaporated when I began to speak"; and "I completely forgot the question I was asked." Our experience of consciousness—the "me" we feel bouncing around inside us—is not a product of the amygdala. Rather, it stems primarily from our learning centers in the brain, the complicated right and left lobes of the cerebellum.

At times of extreme emergency (as defined by the amygdala), the ordinary functioning of the cerebellum gets downgraded so that it does not second-guess or get in the way of imperative bodily responses called for by the amygdala. This downgrading can be intermittent ("I suddenly went blank") or continuous ("I felt like I was in a daze the whole time"). It can result in embarrassing intellectual lapses, such as the temporary inability to form a clear answer to a question.

Perhaps you have personally experienced or observed times when the agenda of the amygdala trumped the ordinary functioning of consciousness and rational thought. For example, a person who responds heroically in a rescue situation may tell an interviewer, "I don't really remember much. It was all a blur. I just did what I knew I had to." An actor wins an Oscar and, in accepting it, proceeds to blurt out ecstatic nonsense that seems wholly atypical of him. A race car driver narrowly averts a disastrous crash and later tells the press, "It all happened so fast. I just reacted." That's the key point, from the point of view of the amygdala: you could react because you had no recourse to thinking, contemplating, debating, and second-guessing.

We have already pointed out that efforts to rewire the amygdala so that it has a friendlier influence on our speaking have been notably unsuccessful. The amygdala will respond to perceived threats today in approximately the same way that it did hundreds of thousands of years ago. The prime directive is still to save the person at any cost. But while speakers cannot guarantee that they will be exempt from occasional mental lapses, they can prepare in advance to deal smoothly and professionally with these annoying moments. A portion of Chapter 1 discusses mental lapses and those who suffer from them.

Message to the Voice

Finally, the primal portion of our brain has remarkable influence on the volume, pitch, and pace of our speaking. Probably because our noble but slant-browed ancestor wanted to make as little noise as possible around the impending tiger, he experienced a choking off of his ordinary vocal volume and huskiness where his dependable vocal cords used to be. In this regard, speakers can often be observed repeatedly clearing their throat in an effort to restore ordinary speaking volume and comfort. Speakers who are told that they talk too softly and need a microphone are the most obvious inheritors of this age-old protective measure forced upon the vocal apparatus by the amygdala. These speakers do not choose to talk more softly when they are nervous; it "just happens," as surely and as naturally as beads of perspiration come to their foreheads or blotches to their cheeks.

With adrenaline coursing through their body, speakers occasionally try to compensate for the small-voice-through-a-soda-straw phenomenon by virtually yelling at their listeners. This volume option, perhaps also evolutionary if it helped chase away the tiger, is no less objectionable to audiences than the soft-voice routine.

Speaker's nerves can also flatten out the normal ups and down in pitch, or musicality, of one's voice. Variation in pitch is a higher-level mental process in which the speaker tries to modulate his or her voice in close coordination with the words being said and with the intended affect on the audience. Vocal variety, in other words, is the hallmark of a thinking, sensitive speaker. But when nerves intermittently or continually degrade the speaker's higher-level mental processing, the otherwise pleasing rise and fall of speaking can fall into a monotone drone.

Pace can also be influenced by speaker's nerves. Because a speaker's "inner reality," as gauged by fast heartbeat and fast breathing, seems to be moving at a whirlwind pace, his or her words may also be delivered much more quickly than in ordinary conversation. Even when a speaker senses the audience isn't keeping up, slowing down can be difficult. "I get on a roll," one speaker reports, "and I don't realize how fast I'm talking. I feel like I'm talking at a regular pace, but the frowns in the audience tell me that people aren't catching half of what I'm saying."

Our Response to Ancient Messages from the Amygdala

Especially when we are in the grip of agonizing speaker's nerves, we feel like shouting to our body (so to speak), "Don't listen to the amygdala! Those messages are all wrong! There's no saber-toothed tiger out there, and I'm not in mortal danger. Quit revving up as if I have to fight or flee. I don't have to do either. It's just a presentation, for heaven's sake, and I'm going to survive—if you will just ease up on the infernal symptoms of speaker's nerves!"

That's exactly the kind of message our conscious, rational mind needs to "say" to itself and the rest of the body. Rational evaluation and reassurance—facing the real situation, not the imagined one—go a long way toward turning off the alarm signals that have been tripped by the amygdala in our hearts, lungs, hands, and so forth. But the process of rationally countermanding messages from the amygdala isn't easy. Our evolution probably has "hardened" these fight-or-flight messages so that they can't be instantly dismissed, the way someone rolls over to hit the snooze button when the alarm clock sounds. The art of calming oneself, and teaching others to regain their cool, involves patience, courage, and not a little trickery (explained in Chapter 4) as we find ways around the powerful alarm circuits genetically hardwired within us.

Summing Up

Like it or not, we modern human beings walk around with a portion of our brain that still reacts automatically to fear stimuli. As much as we might wish to control the amygdala at times, its rapid-fire response to crisis situations probably continues to do us much more good than harm in terms of our chances for survival as individuals and as a species. When we take a moment to realize the power of our primal brain and its apparent intentions in producing the symptoms of speaker's nerves, we begin to cut ourselves some slack. We no longer accuse our bodies of failing us, knowing that the body is doing precisely what our primal brain instructs it to in fight-or-flight situations. Nor do we blame ourselves for not being in complete control of our heartbeat, breathing, perspiration, blotching, and other signs of speaker's nerves. In the same way that early humans could not tell themselves not to react when they encountered a hungry saber-toothed tiger, we do not have a simple on-off switch for our emotional responses to speaking situations. We can, however, develop strategies to make the most of our energy and excitement as speakers. Those strategies are the main subject of Chapter 4.

3

Putting a Face on the Fear of Speaking

In Chapter 2, we saw how powerfully our primal brain, the amygdala, responds to fear sensations from our five senses. We also observed that the amygdala is almost entirely beyond our conscious control. It will invariably set off the bodily alarms it thinks appropriate well before we have a split second to think about the situation at hand—and certainly before we try to decide how we want to respond. A car swerves in the lane ahead of us, and we slam on our brakes, with our amygdala firing out "danger!" messages to the body before our foot can even hit the brake pedal. We react in a split second and save ourselves from an accident precisely because the amygdala didn't give us time to think about the situation.

If we have little control over the amygdala, we may have better luck controlling the stimuli our senses send to that crisis center. With some personal honesty with ourselves, as well as a bit of in-depth soul searching, we may be able to convert our usual fear producers (our tigers, if you will) into tolerable house cats. In short, we can calm the amygdala by not sending it fear sensations in the first place.

But how? The answer requires a complicated but necessary question: What are you afraid of?

Naming Our Fears

When asked what they fear in public speaking situations, some sufferers from speaker's nerves get huffy: "I'm not afraid of anything. I just have speaker's nerves. My mother had them, and her mother before her. It's just a genetic thing, I guess." Or another version: "A lot depends on how well I do. I have every reason to be anxious about a speech I give to a large meeting. It could make or break my career future." And one more: "It's nothing I can name. I'm just shy by nature, and I don't like getting up in front of people to speak."

There's a grain of truth in each of these camouflage statements, of course. Speaker's nerves may have some genetic basis. We are judged by how well we present. And we do have personality tendencies, including shyness, that can explain a portion of our anxiety over speaking. Appendix B presents a personal diagnostic that will help you evaluate elements of your personality that may contribute to certain kinds of speaker's nerves. The easy-to-score instrument gives you the opportunity to get to know yourself better—and, based on those insights, to plan speaking events in a way that aligns well with your main personality features. You may want to turn to this feature of the book now to learn more about how your personality predispositions may be influencing your experience of speaker's nerves.

But whether we have been trying to account for speaker's nerves based on genetics, personality preferences, or other factors, there remains the blunt truth: we are fearful of something in the speaking situation, and we need to give a name and face to that something if we are to put it behind us and move on to more confident speaking.

To do so, the five speakers in the second half of this chapter go into personal and sometimes painful detail about the sources of their fear in a speaking situation. Following the description of each type of fear is specific advice on how to overcome it. Among the five forms of fear described here, you probably will discover one or more sources of fear that resemble your own. The goal in locating such fears is not to isolate weaknesses, character flaws, or failings of any kind. Instead, it is an effort to localize what's standing in your way, see it for what it is, and get beyond it.

Normalizing and Accepting Our Fears

Calming our fears about speaking situations begins by giving fear itself its due as a valuable player in the human condition—in short, accepting fear as more of a friend in our affairs than our enemy. Three examples can make the point:

- You're driving on a straight desert road with no other cars in sight. You've been eager to let out the horses on your new sports car. You press down the gas pedal and watch the speedometer climb to 90, then 100. At 110 the car still feels stable on the road and probably can go even faster. But a feeling at the pit of your stomach tells you, "Fast enough. You're going to feel stupid dying out here when the car flips over." You listen to that voice and slow down, having had your thrill for the day.

- You're enjoying a day at the beach with several college friends. Three are good ocean swimmers. They drag you to the edge of the water and point to a buoy bobbing 200 yards from shore. "The four of us are going to swim out to that buoy. The last one back to shore buys dinner tonight. Come on, don't chicken out. This will be a hoot." You take a long look out to sea at the buoy and decide it's too far for your level of fitness and swimming ability. You bow out of the race but volunteer to be the referee for who touches shore first.

- You're visiting the Grand Canyon with a friend. She steps bravely to the very edge of the canyon, with no safety barrier, and looks down. "Come here, 'fraidy cat. This is unbelievable, looking straight down for a mile!" You begin to walk toward your friend and the edge of the canyon. But when you get about six feet from the edge, you start to feel a touch of vertigo. "This is far enough," you say. "Stay there if you want, but I'll enjoy what I can from back here."

In these situations, did you feel fear? Absolutely. The question is whether you feel you have to apologize for your fear. Unless you are driven to take dares no matter what, you probably are willing to defend your decisions: "Sure, I felt fear. So what? If I never felt fear, I could have died in a car crash, drowned in the ocean, or slipped into the Grand Canyon. If it ever gets to the point where I can't resist the prodding and teasing of my friends to do something against my better judgment, I'll get new friends."

If we accept the usefulness of fear in these real-world situations, why do we have difficulty accepting and even defending the fear we feel in public speaking circumstances? One speaker replies, "Because that fear isn't saving me from anything life-threatening. I'm not in mortal danger while giving a presentation."

The insight here is worth emphasizing: it isn't fear that we need to banish. We're actually quite comfortable with most of our fears and even grateful for them. What we need to adjust is the *proportion* of our fear response, based on the seriousness of the situation—big fears for big threats, little fears for little threats. For those in the grip of speaker's nerves, the dilemma could not be more apparent: we have been cutting butter with an ax by rolling out our most potent, terrible fear responses for speaking occasions that require only a touch of excitement and anticipation.

The goal of this chapter is to show how five individuals whittled down the dimensions of their public speaking fear from big to little, with a corresponding decrease in the symptoms kicked off by their fight-or-flight center, the amygdala (as explained in Chapter 2). Notice that none of these individuals tries to extinguish fear entirely. Instead, they scale it down to reasonable and tolerable size by being as realistic as possible about the nature of the threat involved and their response to that threat.

Common Fears in Public Speaking Situations

What are you afraid of? Anyone who has experienced speaker's nerves needs to confront that question. As explained by the following "true confessions" of speakers, the reasons for fear can range from fear of fright symptoms themselves to fear of making a bad impression to fear of spoiling an idealized plan of some kind. Other speakers fear failure in its various forms or the presence of audience members themselves. None of these fears is "weird" or bizarre; countless thousands of speakers have experienced them—and lived to talk about them here.

Fear of Being Afraid

Cynthia W., a mortgage banker: "What am I afraid of? I think I get nervous primarily because I expect a lot of myself. A speaking experience puts me in the spotlight for better or for worse. I can shine by showing my knowledge and getting the audience to like me. Or I can fail by boring the audience or appearing to be unprepared and nervous. I'm not worried about knowing my stuff; I prepare carefully and don't leave any stones unturned. But my presentations sometimes just seem to go to pieces because I get so nervous. So the main thing I fear at this point is getting afraid. I have worked hard as a woman to get where I am in an industry largely run by men. I've had to project a strong, no-nonsense image to my peers and superiors. When I get up to speak, I'm deathly afraid that all my hard work in creating my solid professional image will crumble as I kind of melt down from nervousness in front of everyone. If I knew in advance that I wouldn't feel uncomfortably anxious, speaking would be a pleasure for me—and probably for my audience as well. But how can I guarantee that I won't show my nervous weaknesses just at the moment in a speech when I'm supposed to be showing my strength and leadership abilities?"

The line from Franklin Delano Roosevelt echoes here: "The only thing we have to fear is fear itself." For Cynthia, the fear she feels when she rises to speak is as palpable and real as the chairs and tables in the room. She worries that "it" will block her efforts to speak effectively and that "it" may be noticeable to her bosses and others in the audience. She wants to get over "it" but doesn't know where to begin.

Cynthia needs to ask, "What is 'it'? Do I really mean 'it,' or am I talking about 'me'? If the latter, then am I somehow trying to get over 'me'?" Once she separates her fear from the rest of her personality and grants "it" status as her enemy, she ends up in the quandary of trying to fight against something that is, in actuality, very much a part of her. Put simply, the "together, strong, and professional Cynthia" is trying to overcome and sti-fle the "sensitive and feeling Cynthia." The battle here is not between Cynthia and speaker's nerves; it's between two parts of Cynthia herself.

The control (or "guarantee") she seeks can come, of course, but not by pitting one part of herself against another part. Cynthia needs to say, in effect, "That's *me* getting nervous in front of an audience. My fears are part of who I am right now." She may hate her nervousness and wish she didn't experience it, but she will have little luck trying to quiet her nerves through the sheer force of willpower. Ironically, the harder she tells her-self, "Don't be nervous, don't be nervous," the more she may find herself in the grip of speaker's nerves.

By analogy, if Cynthia had a broken arm from a skiing accident, let's say, she might hate the pain and inconvenience involved in the injury. But she would not divorce her arm from her sense of herself and her body. She would recognize the problem with her arm, take steps to care for it, and nurse it back to health and usefulness. She would not take unusual measures to hide it completely from others. "They will see I'm wearing a cast," she might tell herself. "So what? Many of them have broken an arm or leg; they know what I'm going through."

Why should emotional distress, such as that involved in speaker's nerves, be any different for Cynthia than an injured arm? She can face up to the fact that she experiences uncomfortable anxiety in speaking situa-tions. Cynthia can strategize, perhaps including counsel from her doctor, friends, and colleagues, to address the problem patiently and effectively. She can resolve to nurse her emotions back into the comfort zone through attentiveness and care, not embarrassment and self-loathing. And while that process is taking place, Cynthia can reassure herself that almost all the people in her audience have struggled one way or another with anxi-eties aroused by public speaking. As noted earlier, speech anxiety remains the most common human fear, outpacing even the fear of death itself, in many large-scale surveys.

Here's specifically how Cynthia confronted her fear of being afraid in front of an audience: "I decided to come out of the closet of speaker's nerves and simply let others know who I was and what I was experienc-ing. The more I tried to hide my nervous suffering, the more it loomed larger and larger as the single biggest threat to my career, my self-image, my reputation, and my happiness. I vividly remember the moment when I dragged my fear of speaking out of the closet and slammed the door behind so I couldn't go back to hiding my feelings. It was about 8:00 P.M. I was watching TV absentmindedly, because my thoughts were already straying to what-if questions about a speech I had to give to about forty customers the next day. What if I get huge perspiration circles on my clothes? What if my voice shakes? What if I go blank? In the middle of these kinds of worries, I caught the tail end of a public service announcement on TV—a woman was speaking about her experience with breast cancer. I can't remember her exact words, but it was something along these lines: 'I don't know why cancer struck me, but I do know that I'm a fighter. I'm not ashamed to lose my hair in chemotherapy. I'm not embarrassed to be nauseous during my treatment. I'm a fighter—and a survivor.' Her brave words and courageous attitude over a problem much more serious than mine made me feel a little silly for getting so worked up over my speaking situation. But her words also awoke in me a new resolve to face up to what I was experiencing and fight back.

"I resolved to try a new tactic. Instead of pretending that I, the superwoman, felt nothing and feared nothing, I decided to try a new strategy at the beginning of my speech the next day. And it worked. I got up to the speaker's podium, looked out at my audience, and told them from the bottom of my heart how excited I was to be speaking to them—excited, I said, even to the point of being scared stiff because I wanted to do the best job possible for them in my presentation. 'So if you see my papers shaking up here,' I told them with a smile, 'you will know that I'm working hard to give you my best shot!' They chuckled and then applauded. I got through the speech just fine, with plenty of excitement and enthusiasm but not the horrible clutch of speaker's nerves. I had converted speaker's nerves into passionate presenting by simply telling people what I was feeling. Once you've admitted to feelings of nervousness, there's not much you can worry about."

Fear of What Others Will Think

Brandon T., a construction company executive: "Public speaking is a big part of getting any big construction project approved by investors, city councils, regulatory agencies, and community groups. I'm the lucky guy who has to stand up, sometimes for an hour or two, and speak to audiences that are often suspicious about the project and people I represent. In the case of town councils and community groups, many listeners are downright hostile. I felt some speaker's nerves when I took this job three years ago, and my discomfort in front of audiences has grown steadily since then.

"Here's my fear in a nutshell. I'm a big guy—six feet, four inches or so—with a booming voice. I come across as strong, assertive, and determined; my nickname around the office is The Bull. I have the reputation of being a 'closer' who can walk into tough situations and come out with a deal. How is it going to look if my hands start to shake when I'm pointing at a diagram on the wall or when sweat starts to drench my collar? If I saw a guy that nervous, I would conclude that he had a lot to hide. The last several times I've spoken before city councils and community groups, I've come away from the experience an absolute basket case. I'm exhausted, sweaty from head to toe, and shaky all over. Some of that had to show during these presentations. In fact, I heard my voice quiver a couple times and quickly coughed to try to cover my nervousness. I mumbled something about getting over a cold. But I don't think I fooled anyone.

"My company needs and expects a confident, emotionally solid representative to make these kinds of important presentations. I'm at the point where I dread such speaking even days in advance. When I walk into the room, I see on people's faces that they are looking for my Achilles' heel, some weak spot to use against me in negotiations. As my nervousness gets worse and worse during my presentation, I can practically see them smiling to themselves and thinking, 'This guy is only pretending to be tough. Look at him; he's shaking.'"

It won't do any good in Brandon's case to tell him not to make such a big deal about the meetings at which he speaks. In truth, they are important to his projects and his company. He is not overestimating the crucial opportunity he has in his speech to make good impressions and move his agenda along to a desired conclusion. He may not have a second opportunity to influence decision makers, persuade his opponents, and negotiate with regulators. Brandon frequently has mentally replayed President Harry Truman's line: "If you can't stand the heat, get out of the kitchen."

Brandon has definitely chosen "the kitchen" for his career. But, he asks himself, can I stand the heat?

Brandon has created his own worst enemy by imputing to his listeners thoughts and motives that may not be there at all. He has convinced himself that all eyes are focused on him, that his slightest bobble or glitch will be seized on by his "enemies," and that any sign of humanness will instantly be interpreted by his audience as a sign of weakness. What an education Brandon would receive if he could get inside the heads of his listeners for even a minute or two. For example, the five city council members supposedly listening to his presentation are primarily thinking about their own issues, interests, and agendas. Member Number 1 has a sick kid at home and wishes he had skipped the meeting entirely. Member Number 2 is thinking about what she wants to say after Brandon is done; she is hardly listening to him. Member Number 3 is angry with Member Number 5 and spends the meeting plotting subtle revenge. Member Number 4 is coming up for reelection and watches the faces of the audience as she thinks about her campaign strategy. Member Number 5 has the beginnings of an ulcer and sits uncomfortably, wishing the meeting would end sooner rather than later. Of course, all tune in and out of Brandon's presentation, so they get the gist of his message. But not a single member is focusing narrowly and ferociously on whether Brandon's hand shakes or whether he is perspiring. Brandon needs to know—and convince himself—that other people are usually thinking primarily about themselves, not him. That realization would let Brandon relax, knowing that he is one player on the stage but not the sole attraction.

Many leading figures in business and government find themselves in Brandon's dilemma. They rise to prominence in their organizations because they command attention, perform well, and demonstrate courage under fire. But these individuals can too easily fall prey to their overblown sense of themselves—their egotism. Perhaps because they expect so much of themselves, people like Brandon come to assume that everyone in the room has similar expectations of them. Speaker's nerves are the body's protest against this kind of overwhelming expectation. Nervous symptoms are the body's way of saying, in effect, "It's impossible to please everyone all the time, and the stress is killing me!"

Here's how Brandon says he achieved a steady reduction in the nervous anxiety he felt in stressful meetings: "I realized I was at the point of inventing reasons why I couldn't show up for an important speaking occasion. One time I used the excuse of my mother's poor health—'a family emergency,' I said. If I went further down this road of excuses, I might as well give up my job and my hopes for promotion. After talking through the problem with my wife and a close friend, I grasped the fact that I was giving entirely too much power to people in my audience by thinking of them as my judges and executioners. In fact, they were just people like me, with all the daily concerns and wandering attention spans that we all have. At my next presentation, I consciously resolved to think of them as friendly, ordinary people, not as mini-gods that held my fate in their hands. In fact, I got to the meeting a few minutes early just so I could shake hands with many of the people and make small talk with them. One guy told me he'd had a flat tire on the way to the meeting. Another was complaining to anyone who would listen, 'You just can't find babysitters anymore. Teenagers just don't want to work, no matter what the pay!' These were just ordinary people. I relaxed and talked to them as friends, not as threats to my career. I can't say that I felt absolutely no nerves during my presentation—and I'm not sure that I would want to speak without any feelings of 'being up.' But I do know that I connected with my audience in a way that I hadn't in many previous presentations. I accepted them for who they were, and in turn, I had the feeling that they accepted me."

Fear of Deviating from "the Plan"

David C., an R&D engineer: "Ever since I was a kid, I have enjoyed designing and building things—model cars, my first home, and now high-end computer systems. It's been my professional experience that almost anything is possible if you think long and hard about the plan you need to follow to get there. For example, my research group was given the task of developing a powerful computer chip so small that it could occupy just a few millimeters of surface space on a consumer credit card. The chip would keep track of account balances while making unauthorized use virtually impossible. For me, the best part of this project was the planning stage. I took the lead in figuring out what we needed to do, who would do it, how we would test it, and how much it would cost. My work group followed that plan to the last detail, and the project came to market successfully and within budget.

"As a result, I got a promotion in my company and now head up the R&D division. In my new role, I have to give briefings and other informational talks to several different kinds of audiences, including the board of directors, Wall Street analysts, and other company divisions. I notice that I get visibly rattled when my speech is interrupted by a question or when my time is cut short by some unexpected situation. I plan my talks very carefully so that points relate logically one to the other. I write out most of my words so that I can communicate as efficiently and accurately as possible. Everything goes fine if the audience just sits back and lets me give my speech as I had planned. But if I'm interrupted by questions or comments, I feel like a train suddenly lurching off its tracks. I have trouble refocusing, my face blushes red, and my voice gets shaky. I don't really feel OK until I've found my place again within my script. I usually tell my listeners that I will take questions at the end of my talk, but they interrupt anyway—especially my bosses in the room. And I can hardly tell them to keep quiet until I have finished what I have planned to present. I feel myself get tight as a drum if the schedule gets changed at the last minute so that I don't have enough time to give my presentation exactly as I planned it. Even a room change can throw me off, especially when I've practiced my presentation in one room and am then told to give it in another room. Is it too much to expect that people will stick to the time, place, and topic they announced in the first place? That's the only way I can give a presentation with any confidence."

David is every parent's dream. As a child, he kept his room clean and well organized. As an adult, he is no less fastidious. His lawn is well manicured, his office is precisely arranged, and even his clothing is buttoned down and coordinated. On the Speaker's Personality Instrument in Appendix B, he scores extremely high as a Planner. For such a no-surprises person, being at the mercy of speaker's nerves has been an appalling experience. Painful, embarrassing attacks of anxiety while giving a speech were definitely not part of David's plan. He tends to blame others as the cause of his nervousness: *they* interrupted, *they* changed the schedule, *they* couldn't wait with their questions, and so forth. He sees his own actions as wholly satisfactory: "I created an excellent presentation plan, and I followed that plan. There's nothing more I could have done to ensure the success of the presentation. They messed it up."

Not quite, David. For all his skill in planning, David has yet to learn the value of spontaneity, flexibility, and willingness to shift gears when necessary to adjust to changing situations. His plan, for all its logic, is fragile in the real world. It falls to pieces at the first unexpected ripple, like a boat designed for ideal weather and sea conditions but vulnerable to the first squall. Disturbances of the sort that make David nervous are hardly the fault of his audience. From the perspective of the audience, spontaneous questions and comments are not an effort to destroy David's presentation. If anything, these expressions of interest are a sign that the audience is involved in what David is saying and wants to know more.

The resolution of David's torment by speaker's nerves does not lie so much in giving up all planning but instead involves realizing that several roads can lead to Rome. David has fixated on one thought path to achieve his communication goal. If he broadens his view to include other possible paths, some of them created on the fly, speaking will become more of an enjoyable challenge than a minefield of possible interruptions.

Here is David's analysis of how he overcame his speaker's nerves and his obsessive need to overplan his presentations: "My breakthrough came at a time that I thought was the worst moment of my life. I was giving a presentation to a group of about fifty managers at a convention in Chicago. I was about two-thirds of the way through my presentation, when my company CEO walked into the back of the room. He listened for a minute or so and then raised his hand. I hated to stop the flow of my presentation, but I had to call on him. He was the big boss. 'David,' he said, 'I just have a few minutes before I have to head to the airport. But if you don't mind wrapping up your presentation right now, I would like to take the remaining time to hear what this group has to say about our latest advertising campaign. Kind of an impromptu focus group, OK?' Obviously, I went along with his request, wrapped up my presentation in a couple of sentences, and slunk away from the podium, feeling I had done a terrible job, all due to his interruption.

"But much to my surprise, at least half a dozen audience members came up to me later to tell me how much they liked my presentation and especially how much they appreciated my willingness to cut things short for the unexpected session with the CEO. I was dumbfounded. They didn't care at all that I hadn't read every page of my presentation and hadn't gotten to every frame of my PowerPoint slides. In fact, they didn't know what they had missed and didn't care.

"What I got from that whole experience—and what has calmed me down considerably since then in my presentations—is that only I, as speaker, know the 'whole enchilada' that I am prepared to present. If I don't get to the whole thing, or have to condense it or change it somewhat, the audience has no clue about these alterations and certainly doesn't hold them against me. What they do hear has to hang together, of course, but it doesn't have to have the exact number of points, tables, and graphs that I had planned in advance to present. In fact, I've gotten kind of hooked on this flexibility thing. I kind of like the creativity involved in having to change things around unexpectedly to fit a new schedule, a different mix of audience, or a change in location."

Fear of Failure

Wendy E., an interior designer for commercial space: "By the time I was twelve years old, I knew what I was good at and what I wasn't. Drawing, painting, and furnishings were my passion even then. I had a gift for picking interesting colors and making good design decisions for the interiors of buildings and homes. What I couldn't do was stand up and give a speech of any kind. In fact, some of my worst school memories have to do with the horrible stomach cramps and nausea I felt before and during my required speeches in various high school and college classes. I resolved to find an occupation where communication was one-on-one, not one-to-many. Especially in my first years as an interior designer, that career suited me perfectly. I met with clients individually or in small groups. I never had to give formal presentations to larger groups.

"But a bittersweet surprise happened along the way: I became successful. Now I am a partner in a large design firm that does interior work for banks, hotels, and civic buildings. In the past year I've had to give seven major presentations by myself to client audiences that have ranged from fifteen to fifty people. To say that I was nervous is to put it too mildly. After my first presentation, I rushed to my doctor to see if I was suffering from an ulcer. My stomach hurt terribly just before and during my presentation. The pain left as soon as my presentation ended. Not surprisingly, my doctor couldn't find any physical ailment. He attributed my pain and digestive upset to stress.

"When I try to name exactly what upsets me when I give a presentation, it's virtually everything. I hate my squeaky, quiet voice. I have lousy eye contact. My gestures are almost nonexistent, since I clutch the podium for dear life. My audiences never smile or react in any way when I'm speaking, though they do give me a scattering of polite applause when I'm done. Probably they are really clapping for themselves for enduring my speech. As I mentioned at the outset, I am just a poor, poor public speaker and always have been.

"The speaker's nerves I feel are comparable to the nervousness a person would feel going up to bat in a major league game if he had never played baseball before. I'm sure I'm going to fail as I walk up to the podium. Even though I manage to get through my presentation, I never feel good about it afterward, and I'm pretty sure my audience doesn't either. I'm just not a public speaker. But I can't go backward by avoiding speeches at this point. It would be letting my firm and my fellow partners down. I'm scared stiff that my repeated failures to give a good speech will keep me from advancing in my career."

If you were observing one of Wendy's professional speeches and then giving her a score, it would no doubt be low. She has made up her mind that she can't speak well before an audience, and her lackluster performance probably reflects her attitude. How do you convince a person dead set on failure that she can give an acceptable and even admirable business presentation?

One approach practiced by some of the best executive speech coaches is to clarify the crucial difference between a talk and a speech. Wendy never said she can't talk. In fact, she is quite charming in person and remembers with pleasure the countless times in her career when she conversed with individual clients for hours about their needs. Wendy needs to realize that personable, sincere talking is perfectly acceptable in almost all professional situations. She has been trying to give a formal speech of the sort assigned to her in high school and college and, as a result, has experienced severe anxiety in the form of speaker's nerves. If Wendy were to forget about "speaking" and tried simply to talk to her audience, she might feel much more successful as a communicator. And with those feelings of success will come a dramatic reduction in the symptoms of speaker's nerves.

Here's how Wendy says she transformed herself from a self-diagnosed failure into a professional who can talk convincingly and sincerely to audiences of any size: "Call it a happy disaster or serendipity. I had reluctantly accepted a speaking invitation at a luncheon across town. Thirty or so architects were gathering—a good chance to tell them about our approach to interior design and maybe attract new clients. Plagued already by the beginning of speaker's nerves, I sat down and wrote out every word of a thirty-minute presentation. My secretary typed it up for me in a large font with plenty of white space between the lines. 'All I have to do,' I told myself, 'is read what's on the page. There's nothing to be scared about. You're totally prepared.'

"I grabbed a cab for the drive across town. Traffic was worse than usual, and I realized I was running a few minutes late. When the cab finally got me to the restaurant, I jumped out and hurried toward the meeting room—only to realize, in a sudden bath of cold sweat, that I had left my presentation script in the cab, now long gone down the street. What was I going to do? The architects were expecting a luncheon speech, and there was no way to cancel at this last moment. I steeled myself for the only option: getting up and talking to them about my approach to interior design and the projects my company is involved in.

"I will admit that I was almost totally unnerved by getting up in front of a group without a carefully prepared script in my hand. But I did it. After a couple of minutes, I felt like I was having a conversation with my audience and not giving a formal speech at all. A few minutes after that, I could have pinched myself: this wasn't a disaster after all, but a relatively pleasant experience. Members of the audience were engaged in what I was saying, eager to ask questions and give their own experiences. The thirty minutes flew by. Afterward, many of the architects came up to thank me for talking with them and exchanged business cards for further contact.

"That evening, I was still shaking my head. Was presenting really this easy and enjoyable after all? Had I been making myself miserable over 'speeches' for nothing?"

Fear of Crowds

Richard B., a pharmaceutical executive: "Because of my work, I know several prominent physicians and psychiatrists. I've now been to three of them as a patient to try to relieve my intense fear of crowds. My doctors say I don't have agoraphobia, the form of panic aroused for many people by crowded, enclosed places. But if you put more than eight to ten people in a closed room to hear me speak, I melt down like ice in a skillet. Last Thursday, for example, my boss asked me to prepare a five-minute talk for 'a few guests' who would be touring our manufacturing facility. I prepared the talk and walked into the company conference room to find, to my horror, more than eighty people waiting to hear me speak. If my boss had told me I would be speaking to a large audience, I certainly would have feigned illness or made up another kind of excuse to get out of the chore entirely. I've had to make many similar emergency exits from uncomfortable speaking situations in the past. In fact, I've gotten pretty good at it. My excuses have ranged from migraine headaches to laryngitis to sick relatives.

"I make up such stories as a way of avoiding some awful symptoms. When I look out at a large crowd and feel my rising adrenaline and incipient panic, my bladder fills almost instantly, and I end up squirming my way through my speech as quickly as possible so I can hurry out to the restroom. I'm also plagued by a fast, thumping heartbeat when I try to speak to crowds. I feel my heart hammering in my upper chest and throat. It feels like it is about to explode. Obviously, I've been to urologists and cardiologists to check out my physical health. They tell me it's just stress. I don't like the way they say 'just.' It's nothing trivial to me.

"None of this happens when I'm giving my weekly management briefing to my work team of seven people. We're all friends, and I can look them in the eye without feeling nervous or 'on stage.' But as the number of listeners rises, so do my speaker's nerves. I'm positive I could not speak to an audience of more than a hundred. I would pass out or have to stop in the middle of my presentation and rush from the podium to the men's room.

"What am I afraid of? All those faces looking at me—and the shocked expressions those faces would take on if (or when) I started feeling really uncomfortable with my bladder problem and panicking over my rapid heart rate. I'm simultaneously worried about a large audience scaring me and that I would scare them by a panic attack or physical breakdown of some kind. I can almost picture them looking at one another and murmuring, 'There's something wrong with him. Is he having a heart attack or a stroke? And why is he squirming that way?'

"What upsets me about large crowds is my inability to figure out how I'm doing in my speech. Some listeners look bored. Others are looking around the room, not at me. A few look like they're snoozing. In small groups, this rarely happens. We give one another the courtesy of listening, or at least pretending to listen. But when speaking to a crowd, I quickly feel overwhelmed by the negative signals being sent to me by so many faces in the audience. I try to look away from particularly inattentive or scowling faces to regain my confidence, but it seems that wherever I look in a large audience, at least a few faces are telling me that my speech stinks."

Richard's experience is common among presenters who suffer from speaker's nerves. "I'm not afraid of speaking," one presenter says. "I'm just afraid of speaking to people." The tipping point that separates a comfortable audience from a frightening audience seems to hover around twelve for most speakers. When a dozen or fewer people are in the room, a speaker has the ability to determine (through interpretation of facial expressions, posture, and so forth) the general level of rapport with the audience. But as that number mounts beyond twelve to twenty, thirty, forty, and perhaps to a hundred or more, a speaker can feel less and less in control of the situation. He or she can't "read" so many faces all at once. The speaker's confidence collapses as he or she begins to worry about how he or she is coming across for the audience—and to worry as well about his or her inability to assess the audience's feelings. The speaker starts to generalize about the negative impressions that "they," the whole audience, are forming about him or her. If a couple of people in the back are talking to one another instead of listening, the speaker interprets that chat as a sign that the entire audience is bored.

Here's how Richard says he learned to speak comfortably to larger and larger audiences: "After one particularly discouraging bout with speaker's nerves at a company meeting, I took a long walk to try to figure out exactly what was distressing me. I tried to determine why I could speak comfortably to a few people and not to a large group. It came down to a feeling of personal contact. With just a few people, I could look at each person and, depending on their facial expressions and body language, adjust what I was saying or how I was saying it. I could speed up or slow down, get more technical or more general, throw in anecdotes or stick to major points—it all depended on the cues and clues I observed in the people before me.

"But when I tried to be sensitive in this way to a larger audience, I quickly became overwhelmed by their feedback. I was trying to mentally process the nonverbal signals being sent to me by dozens of people at the same time. My frustration in this effort came out in the form of speaker's nerves.

"Obviously, I don't have the freedom to send people out of the room until the group is small enough for my comfort level. However, I do have the option of where I direct my own focus as I speak. Here's what I mean. In attempting to speak to large groups, I typically would let my eyes wander quickly over the entire room. That was my mistake. In doing so, I became conscious of dozens of faces in rapid succession. I couldn't take in that kind of massive feedback. I changed my eye contact habits by focusing on only one person at a time, starting with the friendliest face I could find in the audience. By looking at only one person for three or four seconds before moving on, I limited my awareness to just the feedback signals that face was sending me. I found that by choosing individual faces distributed across the entire room, I could give the impression that I was looking at the whole audience, while in fact I was really looking at only one person at a time.

"Almost immediately, I felt a lessening of speaker's nerves, a welcome relief that has continued to the present. I managed to take what I did well—talking to individuals—and applied it to speeches I had to give to larger groups. The key to my escape from speech anxiety lay in one principle that I have repeated often to myself before speeches: 'Even the largest audience is made up of individuals. Talk to them one at a time.'"

Speaker's Nerves as an Exit Strategy

Using internal scripts to resolve speaker's nerves presumes that we are willing to tell ourselves the truth in such personal messaging. We should at least raise the possibility that our supposed fear of public speaking masks another, deeper source of discontent. For example, we may hate our jobs but only feel that antipathy in the form of speaker's nerves when we rise to speak at a company meeting. In this case, getting over speaker's nerves does nothing to address the deeper issue of hating our job.

We all have life experiences that we dread—let's say, Thanksgiving dinner with the disapproving in-laws, an uncomfortable medical procedure, or a hot afternoon stuck in gridlocked traffic. And we have each probably developed coping strategies to help us through these events: "It's just one dinner a year, and they get a kick out of seeing the kids"; "The colonoscopy sounds awful, but my doctor says it's better than risking cancer"; "I may as well turn on the radio and listen to a ball game. This traffic is going nowhere for a while." In short, we learn to talk ourselves into, through, or out of life's pinch points.

Some people who suffer from speaker's nerves have an additional arsenal of such exit strategies. These people often are the last to notice that their attacks of speech anxiety occur at suspiciously convenient times. Dan has been tabbed by his boss to take a business trip far from home to give a speech at an industry convention. The day before the trip, Dan experiences heart palpitations and breathlessness, with accompanying fears that send him to the emergency room. As in the past with Dan's spells, these symptoms upon examination can't be traced to any physical cause. But Dan nevertheless phones in sick with the explanation that he must miss the business trip while he undergoes a cardiac workup (his fourth in the last three years). Dan's phobic fears regarding his heart have become an unconscious exit strategy for career obligations he wants to avoid.

Let's step away for a moment from the specific situation of public speaking to consider a closely allied case that sheds valuable light on the syndrome of social fears. Barbara, twenty-four years old, has a blind date coming up. It sounded like a fun idea last week when her roommate arranged it, but now that only a couple of hours remain before the guy shows up at the door, Barbara is feeling familiar sensations of queasiness. She vividly remembers that at her twelfth birthday party, she had felt suddenly ill and had proceeded to vomit uncontrollably onto the party table and some of her guests.

In the years following, this episode—which Barbara recalls with everlasting embarrassment—has replayed itself a thousand times in her head, particularly at moments when she finds herself socially "on stage," whether at a party, on a date, or in a job interview. At these moments, she has felt that she might vomit, and as she has focused on her fears of throwing up, her feelings of queasiness have increased. Sometimes she had to leave the room to get a drink of water or to sit quietly in the bathroom until the feeling subsided. At other times, she made up lame excuses about recent illness with food poisoning or stomach flu. She has experimented with antinausea medications without positive result.

The blind date knocks at the door. Barbara feels herself bathed in perspiration as she opens the door. "I'm so sorry," she says. "I have to cancel because I'm just not feeling well. I would have called, but it came on so suddenly. I had Chinese food for lunch, and I think it may be food poisoning." The young man graciously accepts her explanation and wishes her well—maybe a rain check for some other time. Barbara sighs with relief as he walks back to his car. Within a few minutes, she is feeling fine again, and in fact orders a pizza for her own dinner.

What's going on here? From an outside view, Dan and Barbara are obviously using their fear responses as excuses to avoid certain experiences. But consider the situation from their points of view. If we confronted them with the evidence that their symptoms tended to occur in suspicious connection with events they disliked, their response might be as follows: "My symptoms are real. I'm not imagining my heart beating fast (Dan) or horrible feelings of nausea (Barbara). You may think it's all in my head, but it's certainly not."

We could call this response the "neurotic equation":

$$\text{Real Symptoms} = \text{Real Threats}$$

Dan and Barbara believe that the absolute reality they feel regarding their symptoms automatically means that the threats associated with those symptoms are equally real. Put another way, the reality of their feelings convinces them of the reality of their perceived threats. A woman with dog phobia does not say to herself, "There's a dog that has no particular interest in me. The chances that I will be attacked are very slight." (This version of the situation would, for most of us, accord with reality.) Instead, the woman runs a long-practiced phobic script something like this: "I'm feeling fear when I look at that dog. Therefore, the dog must be getting ready to attack me. Dogs sense fear, and if I don't get out of here now, that dog will probably start moving toward me. The more I'm afraid, the more the dog will become hostile toward me." Notice here that the felt reality of the symptoms (panic and dread) get projected onto the perceived stimuli, in this case, the dog. A vicious cycle ensues. The more the woman believes that the dog will harm her, the more acute her symptoms of panic and dread become. The more acute her symptoms, the more the woman attributes her fears to the dog.

Breaking the neurotic equation involves inserting a does-not-equal sign:

$$\text{Real Symptoms} \neq \text{Real Threats}$$

At some point, for example, the woman with dog phobia must learn to say to herself, "I am feeling panic and dread, but those symptoms have nothing to do with the dog across the street. My symptoms will gradually decrease the more I see the dog as just a dog, not as a potential monster pursuing me. If the dog does begin to chase me, I have several ways I can get away from it."

The same logic applies to speaker's nerves. A sufferer at the podium can think, "I am starting to experience symptoms, but these do not mean that I am threatened in any way. I'm safe up here, I know my material, and I'm going to give a great presentation. A few symptoms are not going to get in my way."

Summing Up

Calming our fears about speaking situations begins by respecting fear as a necessary and often lifesaving way of responding to threats and emergencies. Speaker's nerves arise when the fear response grows out of all proportion to the stimuli that provoked it. We need to reestablish perspective and proportion by defining exactly what we fear in speaking situations. Five common fears are treated in this chapter:

- **Fear of being afraid.** Some people feel the symptoms of speaker's nerves so acutely that they learn to fear the symptoms themselves, rather than any actual threat or danger involved in giving a speech.

- **Fear of what others will think.** It's tempting to make assumptions about the impression we are making on others and the possible judgments they are making about us. Such presumption is usually off the mark. We would fear the judgments of others less if we realized they are probably focused more on their own concerns than on us.

- **Fear of deviating from "the plan."** Speakers sometimes overly organize their content and delivery to the point that any change in audience, schedule, or location throws them into a dither of nervousness. Flexibility in adapting one's speech to changing circumstances not only is necessary at times but also can prove to be enjoyable as an exercise of creativity.

- **Fear of failure.** Even the most pleasant stroll can be ruined by a constant worry that each step risks injury. Thinking only about ways in which a speech may fail is a sure recipe for disaster. Focus instead on what you can do well in the speech.

- **Fear of crowds.** The experience of speaker's nerves is often amplified by the presence of relatively large audiences. No matter how large, however, these groups are still composed of individuals. By directing eye contact to one person at a time in a large group, the speaker limits the amount of feedback he or she has to process and thereby also controls anxiety arising from too much feedback.

Also, surface symptoms of speech anxiety often mask deeper issues of discontent and unexpressed anger. Hating one's job, for example, can express itself in the form of speaker's nerves — the body's way of screaming out, "I don't want to be here, and I don't want to be doing this job!" Any resolution of such symptoms has to address these deeper causes. Speakers can use a variety of distraction techniques — "tricks" they can play on their own mind to break the cycle of nervous worry (with one symptom begetting a nervous response that brings on additional symptoms, and so on). Distraction works well for relief from speaker's nerves and the rebuilding of confidence because the mind cannot simultaneously focus on its worries while also performing the distracting activity chosen by the speaker.

4

Eight Solutions to
Conquer Speaker's Nerves

If you skipped ahead to this chapter, you're in good company. Anyone who has experienced the pain and possible embarrassment of speaker's nerves is understandably eager to find "the answer." The wide variety of solutions suggested in this chapter makes one important point: your answer to the certain irritation and possible agony of speaker's nerves may be quite different from someone else's. The key to finding that answer lies in searching carefully and patiently through a collection of remedies that have worked for hundreds of thousands of other speakers over the years.

Which answer will work for you? Frankly, no one can say at the outset. You need to select from among possible ways to conquer speaker's nerves and then try them out. After all, you know better than anyone else how you tend to control or reduce other moments of anxiety in your life unrelated to public speaking. As you read through the following list of possible solutions, you may want to begin your experimentation with techniques and remedies that have worked for you in other areas of your life.

Above all, be patient in trying out ways to resolve your speaker's nerves. You may already have invested a great deal of emotional energy over the years in training yourself to expect (and therefore experience) a bout of speaker's nerves whenever you rise to express yourself in a group. You can undo such training, but only with patience and determination.

Starting with Your Physician

You should begin any recovery from speaker's nerves by checking out your symptoms with your physician. Because the general symptoms of speaker's nerves are so familiar, it's tempting to assume that rapid heartbeat, fast breathing, heavy perspiration, shakiness, and all the other symptoms described in Chapter 1 are due to speech anxiety and nothing more. And you may well be right in this self-diagnosis. But recognize that these same physical symptoms may also be caused by a wide range of ailments and conditions that your doctor should rule out before you undertake many of the other solutions described here.

For example, as part of a standard physical examination, your doctor may test you for thyroid abnormalities, heart problems, hypertension, blood sugar irregularities, and other possible explanations for your nervous discomfort. (You can find a full overview of what to expect in Chapter 5.)

In addition to this consultation on your physical health, you may also want to seek advice and counseling from a mental health professional. Again, the suggestion to consider the services of a psychiatrist, psychologist, or psychiatric social worker is not to say, inaccurately, "You must be mentally ill if you're experiencing speaker's nerves." The great majority of people who suffer from speech anxiety manage to find their own solutions without the involvement of a mental health professional. But recognize that these doctors are trained specifically to deal with panic, anxiety, fears, and phobias. Don't discount how valuable they may be to you in speeding your recovery from speaker's nerves and your return to confident, enjoyable public presenting.

Solutions for Consideration and Experimentation

The following solutions to the agony of speech anxiety are "tried and true" in the sense that many people who suffer from speaker's nerves have found them valuable as routes to confident, comfortable presenting. They do not appear here in order of importance or popularity; the eighth solution is no less potent in its effects than the first. Only you can determine which solution or combination of solutions offers the best, most direct path to inner peace and outward confidence when you next approach the speaker's podium.

Preparation and Practice

Many speakers find that the more they prepare a presentation, the less likely they are to experience speaker's nerves. Here's how one manager put it: "I thought I prepared reasonably well for my presentations. I typically made up a set of PowerPoint slides and used them as my outline for what I had to say. But as my speaker's nerves got worse, I realized that my PowerPoint bullet points weren't providing the degree of preparation I needed to feel secure in front of an audience. I started to write out a script of my actual words for my presentation, not just its bare-bones outline. I had that script in front of me in case I got stuck for words or got thrown off track by an unexpected question. Even though I don't read word for word from my script, just having it there on the podium helps me relax. In a way, it's my security blanket. I can look down at any time to find familiar, well-rehearsed words instead of relying on myself, as I used to, to make up the specific words to say on the spot."

Writing out a complete script for an extended presentation takes time and effort, of course. You may find that writing out a detailed set of notes (instead of an actual word-by-word transcript) gives you enough confidence that you won't get stuck in your presentation. The only way to discover if script or note preparation relieves your speaker's nerves is to try these remedies. Begin with detailed notes, perhaps including not only your major points and examples but also specific starter phrases you can use to keep yourself confidently on track. If these detailed notes don't help you regain your composure and increase your enjoyment in presenting, you can ramp up your preparation in the direction of a complete script of what you want to say.

Here's an example of detailed notes for a presentation on the rise of real estate values in a major U.S. city. This example includes only the first note card of the ten prepared by the speaker:

> *What does it mean for students just graduating from college when the least expensive homes in San Francisco cost, on average, $650,000? [The speaker writes out the exact words he plans to use to open the speech.]*
>
> - *Can't expect to save enough for down payment, typically 20 percent ($130,000), no matter how hard they try*
> - *Pay higher federal and state taxes because they don't have a home interest deduction; makes saving harder*
> - *End up with hours of commuting each day if they decide to buy a less expensive home out of the metropolitan area (effect on family life)*
> - *Often have student loans to pay off, which prevents saving for a house down payment*
> - *Home prices keep rising faster than they can save for a down payment (example: $650,000 house inflates to $800,000 in two years, requiring the down payment to go up by another $30,000)*
>
> *Anecdote: "Let me tell you the story of Bill and Ann Fredericks, both in their twenties and recent B.A. graduates from San Francisco State . . ." [Speaker reminds himself how to start an anecdote he knows well.]*

Be forewarned: just writing out detailed notes or even a complete script does not in itself guarantee that you can count on delivering those words and ideas well. Preparation means rehearsing the *use* of your notes and script until you feel ready to speak with confidence. Such rehearsal works best when the speaker doesn't simply do a "mumble run-through" of the speech, saying the words half aloud in an empty room. Instead, give the presentation in the full voice and volume you plan to use with a real audience. If possible, find a willing friend to listen to your dress rehearsal. T. S. Eliot's famous line applies well to rehearsals for presentations: "Between the conception and the reality falls the shadow." Many hapless speakers have enjoyed the idea of a wonderful presentation in their minds, only to face the harsh reality, in front of real people, that their conception was only a pipe dream. They failed to try it out to see if it would fly.

How unfortunate, when it comes to the mental productivity involved in public presenting, that we do not use the commonsense inspection techniques employed in the manufacture of everything from chips to church bells. No professional would feel awkward putting his or her work through a series of tests and inspections (often performed by others) before sending them out to the marketplace. But when it comes to the workmanship involved in presentations, we become needlessly private and shy about our product. We don't want anyone to hear it until its public debut—and too often, therefore, its public failure. Presentations, as mental products, are a matter of craftsmanship. In the same way that a carpenter does not let ego prevent a building inspector from looking over his work, so a presenter should not hide his or her creation (albeit of words, not wood) from the helpful review of others.

Impromptu Techniques

For all the good things that can be said for preparation and rehearsal as ways of relieving speaker's nerves, the opposite of thorough preparation must also be given its due. Perhaps 80 percent or so of all presenters find that their confidence rises as they nail down and practice each point and the exact words of their presentation. But a vocal minority, the remaining 20 percent of presenters, have found that thorough preparation can make speaker's nerves worse, not better.

Here's how an Omaha insurance manager describes her experience with detailed preparation: "I took the time to write out every word of a fifteen-minute presentation to my company's executive committee. When I rose to give the speech, it felt canned and insincere. I kept stumbling over words because I felt like I was reading rather than speaking. I looked down at my script much too often, instead of giving eye contact to members of the executive committee. I felt more and more nervous as I realized that my presentation was not going well. It was correct, but not memorable or persuasive. I had made the mistake of bringing my words to the meeting but not myself.

"The next time I had to give a presentation, I purposely decided to underprepare. I thought about my audience and what they probably wanted from me. And I gave a little thought to the general order of my ideas. But I didn't try to pin down exact phrases or even a rigid order for my points. Instead, I relied on the fact that I knew my job and my material very well and that I could speak clearly and personably about any topic within my area of responsibility. The difference was day and night, as many members of my audience told me after my presentation. I relaxed and found myself conversing with my audience instead of lecturing them. Interest was high in the room, because the audience realized that I was willing to take my presentation in any direction that they wanted and needed it to go. My own energy and excitement level were high; I had to be on my toes and in the moment in order to go with the flow of discussion. But I wasn't nervous or uncomfortable. In other words, I wasn't fighting myself or trying to be something I wasn't. My audience saw the real me—and that's what I will always continue to bring to my presentation experiences. My way out of speaker's nerves was simply to be myself and give my attention fully to my audience, not to overprepare my words for the sake of polish. At the end of the day, I've found that audiences vastly prefer spontaneity and sincerity to a false effort at polish."

This approach to presenting has been called (sometimes unkindly) "winging it." Are you among the 80 percent for whom the technique will spell disaster or among the 20 percent for whom it will relieve speaker's nerves and enliven presentations? The Speaker's Personality Instrument (SPI) in Appendix B can help you decide without the potential problems involved in trying out impromptu techniques before a real audience. If you score high on the Planner scale (see an explanation of this term following the SPI scoring chart in Appendix B), chances are good that thorough preparation will be most suitable for your control of speech anxiety. In contrast, if you score high on the Juggler scale (also explained in Appendix B), you should experiment with winging it—that is, the impromptu approach to presenting. Perhaps you have been overpreparing your material in contradiction to your personality preferences, with the result of uncomfortable nervousness when you present.

A good venue for trying out impromptu techniques is at the next meeting you attend. Follow the flow of discussion and contribute your ideas without a great deal of forethought. Notice that you are able to think and speak quite well on your feet at such moments. Your words may not be as polished as if you had prepared them in advance, but you gain persuasive advantage and audience interest from the fact that you are speaking off the cuff, sincerely, and spontaneously. You discover that, far from falling apart from lack of preparation, your expression of ideas hangs together quite well and cuts to the chase of what other members of the group care most about. Impromptu speaking has helped you eliminate wordiness in what you are saying.

If you find that you like the person you are in such meetings and are successful in communicating your ideas spontaneously, apply this insight and experience to more formal presentations, perhaps beginning with the next short speech or briefing you give. Think about what you want to achieve and the needs of your audience. Give some thought to possible points you want to make, but not to a rigid order or expression for those points. Rely on your expertise to help you find the appropriate words and the most meaningful ideas at just the right time—a time you cannot predict before the speaking occasion. Then, when you rise to speak, let it flow. Allow your personality, sensitivity to the needs of your audience, and broad background knowledge of your topic to combine into a winning presentation virtually free from speaker's nerves.

In this context, we interpret speaker's nerves as the uncomfortable static that occurs when your true self is at odds with the persona or public image you are presenting. It is as if your inner self protests, "I feel completely phony when I talk this way, and I'm sure my audience members can tell that I'm not being myself." No wonder the body senses danger—psychological and social danger—and reacts with a display of irritating symptoms that makes the speaker feel even more self-conscious and uncomfortable in front of others. Removing the false armor of overpreparation allows the real person to shine through, healing the rift between "who I am" and "who you see me as."

Again, a note of caution: throwing thorough preparation out the window is not the solution for every speaker, or even most. Consider impromptu techniques for speaking as one possible solution among many, not as the cure-all for every form of speaker's nerves.

Environment and Process Imaging

"I thought my speech would go fine, but I didn't expect that spotlight! It made my face drip with perspiration. And the microphone was weird. I kept hearing my voice echoing from the back of the ballroom. The podium was the wrong height for me. When I set down my notes, they were too far away for my glasses. I kept having to stoop over to see them."

This complaint is the lament of a speaker who failed to look over and try out the environment in which he had to give a major presentation. He didn't visit the ballroom before delivering his speech because he had attended a conference there a couple of years before—though as an audience member, not a speaker. He didn't try out the microphone system because the conference facility had an excellent reputation for top-notch audio assistants. He didn't stand in front of the lights on the stage because—well, he never gave them a thought. The net result was one more squirming executive, uncomfortably tugging at his soaked collar as he gutted his way through an awkward presentation, one that did no good for the company or for his reputation.

Speakers can take a valuable lesson from professional athletes and learn to think, feel, and "see" their performance before the actual moment. In ski and bobsled competitions, for example, spectators and TV viewers observe athletes, eyes closed, doing mental run-throughs of their anticipated event. Hours or days before, they took several practice runs down the course. They memorized every bump and turn. In a form of quiet personal gymnastics, they actually move their bodies through silent trial runs of how it will go. And, not surprisingly, they often find remarkable success performing up to the level of their imagined ideal. They don't try to banish excitement, but they do take panic and distressing nervous symptoms out of the equation. They remove negative surprises by imaging their environment and the process of their performance.

Speakers can do likewise by playing through their presentations in advance—and more than once. For example, major speakers at political conventions almost always take the time to stand at the podium, experience the lighting, give at least a portion of their speech, and ask for feedback from colleagues, assistants, and media professionals. Businesspeople often don't take the time for similar imaging of their performance environment. They arrive at the speaking venue along with the audience, instead of getting there well in advance to get a feel for the room, the sound system, the seating arrangement for the audience, and other aspects of their speaking environment. Why? In some cases, the force of habit keeps them from doing what common sense tells them they should. In other cases, their deep-rooted anxieties about speaking keep them away from "the scene of the accident" as long as possible. They don't want to visit the room in advance because they don't want to feel the clutch of nerves in their throat, the early hints of nausea, the uncomfortable quickening of their heartbeat.

These symptoms and all the rest associated with speaker's nerves can be significantly reduced by facing the dragon head-on. Take time well before your presentation to stand up comfortably and confidently in the very location where you worry you will be sweating bullets later in the day. Try out various voice levels and microphone settings to remove any surprises. Imagine yourself looking at audience members in the front row, the middle rows, the back of the room, and along the sides. Let your hands gesture freely as you run through how you expect your presentation to look and sound. This investment of perhaps no more than thirty to forty-five minutes can pay huge dividends in your levels of relaxation, sincerity, and enthusiasm when you rise to give your actual presentation.

Social Assurance

As described in Chapter 3, many fears associated with public speaking have to do with what others may be thinking—or, more accurately, what we guess they are thinking. Ironically, we usually focus on negative judgments our audience may be making, not on what they may be appreciating and applauding in our presentation. This tendency to see the glass half empty instead of half full contributes to our nervous discomfort: we react fearfully to what we imagine in our audience, not to what we actually observe.

Speakers can calm their anxieties about feeling unpopular, ridiculous, or unvalued by literally or metaphorically "making friends" with audience members before the presentation. The clichéd way of establishing this friendly relationship is to tell a joke at the beginning of the speech. The speaker hears chuckles of appreciation from the audience and assumes that he or she is now on good social terms with these listeners. Although humor has a well-earned place in presentations, the practice of always beginning with a joke, no matter how unrelated to the speech at hand, has now become threadbare with audiences. If the joke is told as a pro forma way of warming up the audience, the reaction is as likely to be groans as laughter.

Consider additional ways of feeling comfortable with your audience before you begin to speak. Here are five proven techniques for becoming more confident that your audience likes you and wants to hear you out:

1. Find out in advance who will be in your audience, by level of authority or job responsibility, if not by name. Think through what these people probably want from your presentation. You can feel comfortable in advance about your material if you know it will fulfill your listeners' needs and expectations.

2. Meet with several audience members a day or two before your presentation. Describe your speech, and ask for their feedback. Incorporate their reactions into your revision process before giving the presentation. Above all, enjoy the opportunity to try out your ideas on others in advance of your presentation, and communicate your appreciation for their time and attention. If you can feel valued and in sync with a focus group of this kind, you can carry forward those feelings of acceptance and confidence to your actual presentation.

3. Get to the presentation room early, as audience members begin to arrive. Shake hands with people, make small talk, and work the room without forcing yourself to be less than natural. Feeling comfortable with

audience members on a one-to-one basis gives you a similar level of social confidence when you rise to speak.

4. Keep yourself actively involved in conversation of some kind as long as possible, up to a few moments before you begin your speech. Speakers who insist on sitting silent at the head table, stewing in their own juices of anxiety, only allow their nervousness to build before the high-adrenaline moment of standing up to speak. To dissipate any anticipatory anxiety, chat with others, focusing on their interests and concerns, rather than your what-ifs about the impending speech.

5. Dress in a way that gives you confidence in the presence of your audience. This advice is not intended as the usual "dress for success" pitch. No one can tell you (as many articles and paperbacks try to) what constitutes a "power suit" or "executive accessories." The key point is that *you* should feel fine, or better than fine, about how you've dressed for the speaking occasion. Audiences gain impressions as powerfully and memorably from what they see as from what they hear.

Breathing and Body Work

Under the influence of nerves, our normal breathing patterns go haywire. We find ourselves taking quick, shallow breaths or repeated deep breaths as if we were starving for oxygen. The uncomfortable consequence of disturbed breathing is an imbalance of carbon dioxide in the bloodstream, commonly termed hyperventilation. (The common therapy of having a person breathe into a bag increases the amount of carbon dioxide the person takes in, thereby correcting the imbalance of blood gases.) We feel lightheaded and tingly in our fingers, toes, and cheeks. We may feel suddenly uncoordinated (the familiar image of a speaker knocking over the glass of water on the podium), with a darkening around the field of our vision (the "tunnel effect" reported by many anxious speakers). If we allow panic to make us breathe even faster, we can actually pass out, as Winston Churchill did under the influence of speaker's nerves during his first speech to Parliament. Once we are unconscious, our parasympathetic nervous system (acting as it does without the interference of our rational mind) quickly restores healthful breathing rhythms and normal levels of gases in the blood. After a moment or two, we wake up from hyperventilation feeling physically none the worse for the experience but emotionally shaken. Understandably, fainting has scared not only us but also those around us.

The key to avoiding the distressing symptoms of hyperventilation is to catch it early. At the first symptoms of lightheadedness, tingliness, or darkening of the field of vision, regularize your breathing as follows:

1. Fill your lungs "to the bottom" (although this description isn't precisely accurate physiologically) by pushing out your stomach as you take in air to the count of 1, 2, 3. This technique is called diaphragm breathing, which maximizes the amount of lung tissue in contact with fresh air coming into your body. It is also the form of breathing that occurs naturally during sleep.

2. Hold your breath comfortably to the count of 1, 2, 3.

3. Release your breath easily to the count of 1, 2, 3, so you empty your lungs.

4. Repeat this routine for a dozen or so breaths, making adjustments according to how you feel. Don't hold your breath any longer than is comfortable. Let your count of 1, 2, 3 be only a guide, not a rigid rule. Relax and enjoy your easy, slow, comfortable breathing.

Within a minute or often sooner, this routine will produce several beneficial effects, though not in a particular order. You will feel a general warming across your body, particularly in your palms, cheeks, and major muscle groups. This feeling is associated with a phenomenon termed the relaxation response—a wave of well-being and restfulness that sweeps over the body, replacing the tension of anxiety and muscle tightening. Also, your mind will feel settled and clear—the "centered" response produced by various forms of meditation and yoga involving breathing exercises. Finally, you will feel physically rejuvenated and coordinated. Sensations of lightheadedness and fears of fainting will disappear.

That's not a bad payoff for a minute or so of purposeful breathing! Best of all, you can practice this routine in public without attracting attention to yourself. Many speakers have learned to continue their comfortable breathing exercise in the midst of making small talk with others at the table.

But what can you do if feelings of hyperventilation occur while you are giving your speech? This problem occurs particularly when speakers, under the influence of nerves, rush through their speech, pouring out breath without taking time to breathe in. In physiological terms, they are ridding their lungs of too much carbon dioxide, putting their blood gas level at an imbalance and setting off symptoms of hyperventilation. Admittedly, it's usually not possible to stop for a minute or more in the middle of a presentation for a refreshing, restorative period of 1, 2, 3 breathing.

However, you can recognize that you're pushing out too much breath too quickly. Adjust the pace of your speaking, and allow pauses to fall often, perhaps at the end of each sentence or after an important term or idea. (Your audience will interpret such pauses as a sign that you want them to think about what you just said. They will not know that you are acting to avoid increased symptoms of hyperventilation.) During these pauses, remind yourself to breathe in comfortably and deeply, using the four-step diaphragm breathing technique just described. If you need additional time to restore natural breathing, pause to take a drink of water (it's always a good idea to have a glass of water handy at the podium). Don't hurry yourself. No audience has ever clamored for a speaker to end a pause, although many audiences have wished for a pause—preferably a permanent one from the speaker.

In addition to unobtrusive breathing exercises, a speaker can use unobserved techniques to relax the body and banish muscular tension before rising to speak. Most of the symptoms of speaker's nerves—shakiness, shifting from one foot to the other, inability to gesture naturally, stomach spasms, and so forth—are indicative of tension stored in the muscles. Relieving this tension eliminates the bothersome symptoms and with them the fear of speaker's nerves.

Obviously, a full-body massage would be delightfully relaxing right before a presentation. That's not going to happen in all but the most informal of business environments. Instead, you can practice a well-proven technique for muscular relaxation without attracting attention to yourself:

1. Starting with your feet, tense your muscles there to a slow count of 1, 2, 3.

2. Allow your foot muscles to release and relax, slowly and completely. Don't continue on to the next muscle group until your feet feel drained of all tension and comfortable. If necessary, repeat the tensing/relaxing routine once or twice with your feet before proceeding to step 3.

3. Move upward to the muscles in your calves, knees, and thighs. Tense each of these muscle groups to a slow count of 1, 2, 3, and then allow them to release and relax.

4. Continue this progression of tensing/relaxing major muscle groups upward on your body, concluding with the important tensing and releasing of muscular tension in your neck and face, where nervous energy exerts an especially felt influence. Tensing your face doesn't have to involve contorted expressions. Simply raise your eyebrows, and then let them release and relax. Tense your cheeks, as if in a forced smile, and then let them release and relax.

The net result of this body routine, taking three or four minutes at most to complete, is an overall feeling of deep relaxation and well-being. You have used a form of mental judo—purposely increasing tension in order to remove tension—to put yourself physically and emotionally at ease. When you rise to speak, you do so feeling like yourself, not a frazzled basket of nerves.

Adjustments to Attitude and Frame of Mind

What do you say to yourself, privately and perhaps half consciously, before you give a presentation? Many students admit to focusing on their desire for a good grade: "I've got to get an A on this presentation. I've got to pour everything into it. I've got to bear down and try as hard as I can." When an overwhelming bout of speaker's nerves defeats their best intentions, they wonder in retrospect what went wrong: "I just fell apart. I have no idea why."

When it comes to speaking comfortably and confidently, there is such a thing as trying too hard. Gritting one's teeth, tensing up, and "trying as hard as I can" doesn't work in most sports any more than it works in public speaking. A golfer stepping up to an all-important putt has to set aside do-or-die tensions in favor of relaxation and a natural putting stroke. Similarly in tennis, the shot that causes a player the most stress seldom turns out to be a winner. (Recall how often you have seen a player ferociously rush the net for an overhead slam, only to put it into the net.) The frequently observed phenomenon of "beginner's luck" in bowling, pool, and other sports can largely be explained on the basis of the power of relaxation and the absence of "bear down" attitudes.

Translated to public speaking, the value of a calm, confident attitude has everything to do with relief from speaker's nerves. For example, the student who focuses obsessively on bearing down to get an A would probably be more likely to achieve that goal if he or she thought, before speaking, "This isn't Armageddon. It's a chance to speak comfortably and sincerely to classmates who are my friends and a professor who wants me to succeed. If I get myself too amped up over the grade, I'll tie myself up in speaker's nerves and flub the assignment." In this case, not trying too hard is the key to optimal achievement.

For business and professional people, speaking occasions at major meetings and conventions do often constitute career-changing moments, for better or worse. Performing spectacularly as a speaker in front of company executives can lead to rapid promotion, just as lackluster performance can stop a career dead in its tracks. But what attitude on the part of the speaker is most conducive to spectacular performance? Certainly not the kind of thoughts that keep a person awake at night, sweating over all the details of content and delivery calculated to impress this or that VIP in the audience.

As an alternative to do-or-die, high-anxiety attitudes in such speaking situations, here are four "scripts" (or talks we give to ourselves) that emphasize the importance of relaxation and naturalness over stress and obsessive concentration. Find the script that best suits your personality and circumstances, and then translate it into your own words for the next time you're tempted, metaphorically, to force a putt or rush a swing in your business presenting:

- "Of course the presentation I'm about to give is important to my career. But if I dwell on all the what-ifs, I'll end up so tense that my presentation will be terrible. I'm going to think about this speech as just another presentation. I'm going to try my best, as I always do, but I'm not going to tie myself up by worrying."

- "I can choose to make this speech the most painful experience of my life or one of the most stimulating and enjoyable. I'll choose the latter by thinking positive thoughts about my audience, my abilities, and my future. If good things come from this presentation, that's great. If not, all the nervousness in the world wouldn't have helped."

- "I can do a great job with this presentation by keeping my focus on what I can give my listeners, not on what they think of me. I can't control their judgments, but I can control my efforts to meet their needs."

- "Each person in my audience is glad he or she is not up here giving this speech. Everyone knows what I'm going through. I have no reason to fear speaker's nerves or worry about hiding them, because I know my entire audience has felt speech anxiety in some form. I'm among people just like me. There's no need to feel awkward, isolated, or on display. I can just relax and be the member of the group doing the talking for the period of my speech."

Like physical exercise routines, attitude scripts are most effective when they are repeated regularly. Many traditional forms of meditation make use of a mantra, or meditative phrase, that is repeated over and over until it settles deep into the consciousness as a basic principle of living. In the same way, your personal version of a confidence-building script has to become part of you through repetition. Consider writing down your "message to yourself" on a card and then placing it where you can't help but see it—and think about it—on a daily basis. If this kind of repetition feels awkward at first, recall that you have probably repeated the negative scripts of speaker's nerves hundreds of times to yourself: "It was awful. I felt like I was going to pass out. I never want to feel that again. I hate public speaking. I'll avoid it like the plague." Some speakers have spent years in the echo chamber of such frightening and defeating thoughts. To put speaker's nerves behind you once and for all, you need to perform a transplant operation: out with destructive personal scripts and in with inspiriting messages that lead to confidence, calm, and achievement.

Distraction Techniques

Unlike modern computers, the human mind is not good at parallel processing. For example, we cannot simultaneously worry about the symptoms of speaker's nerves and think about the great hike or bike ride we are going to take after the meeting. One set of thoughts automatically chases out the other.

This insight can be usefully applied to achieving relief from speaker's nerves. We can trick the mind out of its anxiety over an impending speech by forcing ourselves to think of something else, no matter how trivial. Each of the following three techniques uses distraction to banish the symptoms of speaker's nerves and allow the parasympathetic nervous system (the mechanism responsible for the relaxation response) to establish normal and comfortable breathing, heartbeat, blood pressure, perspiration levels, and so forth. Note, however, that for all their effectiveness as short-term solutions to speaker's nerves, these distraction techniques do not get at the deeper causes of our fears before an audience. At best, they provide Band-Aid relief to help us through crisis moments. They don't explain why those crisis moments occurred in the first place.

Distraction by Counting. Coach Lou Holtz of football fame popularized this stress reliever by forcing himself to say the multiplication tables from 1 to 12 during the high-tension hour before the big game (and for Holtz, all games were big games). Keeping his mind active on 9 times 6, 9 times 7, 9 times 8, and on up the number line prevented Holtz's anxiety from taking over and sending him onto the field a nervous wreck.

Multiplication or division tables may do the trick for you before a presentation. Even more effective for many professional speakers and actors is the technique of silently counting backward from 100 by threes: 100, 97, 94, 91, 88, 85, 82, and so on down to 1. The mental work involved in subtracting backward down the number line is just taxing enough for the mind to prevent worrisome thoughts about the upcoming speech from creeping into one's conscious thoughts. This activity works especially well in the last few minutes before a presentation, the time when adrenaline tends to rise precipitously and nervous symptoms start to be felt. You can work through this easy distraction technique without attracting notice from anyone in your audience. A note of caution: Don't make it a race to see how quickly you can complete the count from 100 down to 1. Haste in this case will only add to your stress level. Let the numbers come into your mind lazily, without thinking too hard. With each falling number, let yourself feel your tension level falling as well. (The routine practiced here is not autohypnotism, since you do not enter a trance of any kind. But the use of numbers to direct the attention and lower stress is a familiar technique in many forms of hypnotism.)

Distraction by Connection to a Cherished Object. Talismans and lucky charms are as old as humanity itself. The great majority of the world's population at this very moment clings to some object, symbol, picture, or totem as a way of inviting and fostering good fortune. Although your worldview probably prevents you from clinging to a carved piece of boar's tusk for protection against bad spirits in the jungle, you can at least borrow the distracting power of such a talisman to escape the "bad spirits" of speaker's nerves. Here's how: Select a small object or picture that has deep personal meaning for you—perhaps a key chain one of your kids made for you or a small picture of someone you love or admire. Carry this item with you to the speaking occasion. When you feel nervous symptoms beginning to build, consciously turn your attention to all that the object or picture means to you. Let your mind go back to the days when your child was dashing off to camp. Look at the small picture, and let memories of the relationship flood back into your thoughts and feelings. These brief "mental vacations" from the stressful moments before and during the speech provide the minute or two of distraction necessary for the relaxation response to do its restorative work.

One Northern California grocery executive used this kind of talisman after failing to find relief from counseling and hypnotism to relieve his severe encounters with speaker's nerves. What bothered him most, he said, was the ice-cold feeling in his hands before he started speaking. "Once my hands get cold," he revealed, "I know all the rest of the terrible symptoms are sure to follow." His speech coach made an unusual suggestion: "Let's go down to the sports store and buy a few of those cheap, crushable hand packs that hunters and hikers use to warm their hands in cold weather. Keep one in your jacket pocket. When you feel your hands beginning to get icy, simply reach in and crush the hand pack in your fist. It will radiate 100 degrees or more of warmth for a few minutes. Your hand will feel the heat, and you won't be tempted to automatically slip into the downward spiral of other nervous symptoms."

The executive tried the technique, and it worked. Halfway through an important speech, he felt nervous stress rising again in the form of rapid breathing and a quick heartbeat. He reached unobtrusively into his jacket pocket, squeezed a crushable heat pack, and with its spreading warmth felt the return of his own confidence. In the two years since he began this unusual experiment with an object used for distraction, he has weaned himself off heat packs for all but the most important and stressful addresses he has to give at industry conventions and other large speaking venues.

Another example involves a prominent book agent in New York City. On a dare from a friend, she competed to appear on a TV game show that offered thousands of dollars for correct quiz answers from contestants. An extremely bright and personable woman, she easily qualified to appear on the show. But a horrible thought overwhelmed her: what if her frequent experience of speaker's nerves caused her to go blank, stutter, or otherwise fall apart when the hot lights came on and the TV camera began to roll?

By phone, she confessed her worries to a psychologically savvy friend on the West Coast. Trying to keep from chuckling, he told her as follows:

"Don't worry about anything. I'll FedEx you something that never fails to banish speaker's nerves. It's been used by thousands of speakers for generations. Wrapped carefully inside the FedEx envelope, you will find a small petrified monkey testicle mined from the mountains of Borneo. Tuck it in your purse, and step onto the TV stage without a worry in the world. You are shielded and protected by the powerful magic you know you have in your purse." The friend then went to a local grocery store, brought home a single coffee bean, and expressed it to the agent. When she received it, she laughed at the absurdity of pretending that the coffee bean was in fact a petrified monkey testicle that bestowed magic and protection in any form. Every time she thought about her friend's ruse, she giggled to herself. But she nevertheless stuck the coffee bean into her purse before going into the TV studio for the taping of the quiz show.

She performed brilliantly, winning more than $65,000 over a three-day period with the show. At the end of the experience, she called her West Coast friend again. "I knew it was just a coffee bean. But whenever I felt myself starting to get nervous, I thought about the silly thing sitting in my purse and the whole hype you provided about monkeys and Borneo. The thought made me laugh inside, and that instantly dissolved any nervousness I was feeling. I guess the magic worked after all."

There's no magic in objects or pictures other than the power we bestow on them to take our thoughts elsewhere for a brief, important moment of relaxation. Consider this distraction technique as an unnoticeable way of regaining your composure when the first signs of speaker's nerves appear.

Distraction by Focusing on Aspects of the Audience or Room. Once a speaker grasps the trick of sending attention elsewhere, virtually any interesting point of focus can serve as a stimulus to helpful and temporary distraction. You might decide to look out at your audience to see how many people have dyed their hair or how many men have facial hair or how many women are wearing necklaces. Let your attention bore in on details of the room itself—an odd painting, a strange choice of carpet pattern, an artful use of beams in the ceiling. Count how many lights illuminate the room. Listen carefully for ambient noise—the clatter of lunch plates, the hum of air conditioning, the scrape of chair legs against the tile floor. Any source of focus along these lines can distract your attention away from the nervous symptoms you have learned to expect as a dreaded part of public speaking.

One infamous distraction technique recommends that you imagine your audience naked. That approach stems from the fact that speakers are usually less anxious when speaking to an audience they consider to be inferior to them in some way. When an adult speaks to a kindergarten class, for example, we would not expect him or her to be racked by nervous symptoms of the sort the person might have experienced in a recent speech to his or her company's board of directors. Kindergarten kids offer no threat to the speaker, who knows more than they do, can answer any of their questions, and in the future won't be affected by their opinion of him or her.

But should a speaker make it a regular and necessary practice to imaginatively make others small and ridiculous (sitting there naked, as it were) as the price that must be paid for the speaker's confidence? In other words, must the speaker make you a child to feel that he or she is an adult? In subtle ways, the "imagine them naked" approach backfires in at least three ways:

- The speaker tends to adopt a patronizing or superior tone. After all, he or she is talking to ridiculous people who have no clothes on. The speaker is the only one fully dressed.
- Rapport suffers, as audience members sense that the speaker is not fully present as their equal in the room. (Who would be, given a room of naked people?)
- The technique is harder to practice than one might think. It takes considerable imagination to undress a room full of people in business attire. The sheer work involved distracts the speaker not only from nervousness but also from the text of his speech. More than one speaker has had to admit, "I'm sorry for losing my train of thought. I was busy imagining you naked."

In sum, distraction techniques are best thought of as helpful and temporary bandages for the annoyance of speaker's nerves. They can stop the bleeding, but you will want to investigate deeper reasons for your speaker's nerves to achieve a long-term cure.

Buddy System Approaches

"I couldn't have gotten through this without you." Those words have been spoken between friends in dozens of training situations employing the buddy system: military boot camp, corporate training, conditioning sessions for sports, and so forth. The buddy system can also be extremely valuable in helping people through the worst moments of speaker's nerves.

The insights that led to the use of the buddy system in relation to speech anxiety came from intensive study of people who experience panic attacks. Typically, a panic-prone person tends to locate a "safe" person— often a spouse, sibling, or close friend—who understands the condition and knows what to say and do in the event of a panic attack. The panic sufferer knows in advance that his or her attack will not scare the safe person, nor will that person take unusual and unnecessary rescue measures such as dialing 911 for paramedic support. The safe person can be counted on to patiently, reassuringly talk the panicked person down from the attack. Because of these attributes of the safe person, the panic-prone person rarely has an attack in the presence of this selected companion. Those suffering from panic syndrome often end up dragging their safe people along on shopping trips and business trips as a way of preventing the occurrence of panic attacks ("It won't happen if you come along with me").

The buddy system, as it is used in relieving speaker's nerves, works like this: Two people who suffer from speaker's nerves (perhaps two coworkers) begin their buddy association by having thorough, truthful conversations about their experiences with speaker's nerves. They talk through the awkwardness, fright, and embarrassment they have felt at various times in the grip of speaker's nerves, no holds barred. They commit to observing one another's presentations as an audience member and then being there afterward to talk through whatever nervous symptoms the speaker felt or showed during the speech. This debriefing has the primary goal of reassurance: "You looked good up there. What you were feeling didn't show much at all to your audience. You're making good progress. Your next speech will be even more confident."

Using books like this one, buddies can suggest new techniques to try, in the effort to overcome speaker's nerves. Once a particular technique is under trial, buddies can monitor one another's stick-to-itiveness and possible backsliding: "Are you thinking positive thoughts or negative thoughts about your speech? Have you chosen a distraction technique to try? What script about giving the speech is running in your head right now?"

Buddies can also mark progress and eventual triumph by celebrating successes: "You got through that entire speech without giving in to speaker's nerves. You never could have done that even a month ago. Let's celebrate with lunch out."

In most organizations, it's best for buddies to self-select one another rather than being randomly assigned by a well-intentioned trainer or manager. The buddy system works only when both parties feel a bond of trust, assurance of confidentiality, and mutual empathy for the nervous symptoms they experience.

Summing Up

Solutions to speaker's nerves should be undertaken in a way that includes the evaluation of your physician and/or mental health professional. Once you have received their expert counsel on your symptoms, you can consider one or more of the solutions offered in this chapter.

5

Medical Approaches to
Conquering Speaker's Nerves

THIS CHAPTER EXPLORES medical and psychological options that have proved successful in the treatment of speech anxiety. You'll find a detailed description of what you can expect when you tell a physician or mental health professional about your experiences with speaker's nerves. The goal of this description is to make a doctor's visit less intimidating and confusing. You can take along a copy of the worksheet in Appendix A to show to your doctor and leave as part of your file. This succinct, orderly summary of your nervous symptoms will quickly communicate important aspects of your situation to your doctor.

What to Expect in a Medical Evaluation

Getting a medical evaluation for the kinds of symptoms associated with speaker's nerves is fairly standard, routine, and straightforward. The description that follows is thorough; your own doctor, based on his or her previous knowledge of your health record, may skip some of the evaluation stages explained here.

Many doctors perform a medical evaluation for speaker's nerves or other anxiety conditions in two stages. During the first half of the exam, the focus is on your history. This includes your personal history and habits, such as the details of your occupation, your marital status and education, and whether you drink alcohol, smoke, ingest caffeine in large amounts, use recreational drugs, and so on. You may be asked to fill out short questionnaires designed to elicit any underlying emotional disorders.

Then the doctor focuses on your medical history, including previous medical problems, medications, allergies, surgeries, and health problems in your family. The doctor performs a "review of systems," which is a list of questions about all your bodily functions and complaints. With all this information, the doctor compiles a problem list, which is a summary of your known or previously diagnosed conditions, as well as your undiagnosed complaints. From this list, the doctor then tailors a plan aimed at most effectively getting the answers needed for accurate diagnosis and treatment. The plan may include getting blood work, an x-ray of your chest, a sample of your urine, and an electrocardiogram of your heart for starters. If indicated, the evaluation may include a more in-depth look at the heart with the treadmill stress test, heart CT scan, twenty-four-hour heart monitor, or echocardiogram tests.

Sometimes, a look at the brain is helpful. This is usually best accomplished by MRI scans to look at the structure of the brain. Other brain scans, known as SPECT scans, can give information on brain metabolism and function. If your doctor suspects a well-established phobia as part of your condition with speaker's nerves, some of the important labs and tests he or she may order include the following:

- Thyroid function tests, looking for high or low thyroid performance
- Fasting glucose, looking for low blood sugar, or hypoglycemia
- Calcium level, looking for an overactive parathyroid gland causing high calcium levels

- Cardiac enzyme tests, especially if you have chest pains and heart palpitations
- Drug screen, if illicit drug use is suspected (your physician will ask your permission for this)
- Twenty-four-hour urine for 5-hydroxyindoleacetic acid (5-HIAA) levels, looking for an internal tumor called pheochromocytoma that secretes stress hormones
- Head CT scan—a computerized three-dimensional x-ray designed to identify any structural abnormalities in your brain
- MRI scan—a scan that does not use radiation but uses nonionizing electromagnetic energy to image the brain and spinal cord
- Echocardiogram, which uses sound waves to produce an image of the heart structures, especially looking for mitral valve prolapse, a condition that can cause heart palpitations
- ECG or twenty-four-hour Holter monitor (to exclude heart damage or arrhythmias)

When all the tests are completed and results received at the office, the doctor then brings you in for the second half of the exam. In this session, the doctor goes over all your results and gives you copies for your personal file. Then the physician does a routine physical exam appropriate for your age and complaints. After all this is done, a new problem list is generated, adding on new findings from the tests and physical exam, if any. Finally, a specialist may be called in to give an opinion on a specific question. The specialist might be a neurologist, cardiologist, psychiatrist, endocrinologist, or any of a variety of other physicians with special insight and expertise. Often, no other special tests or specialty consults are necessary, and the doctor is ready to decide on a treatment plan for medical intervention.

Working with Your Doctor

To make this medical workup as accurate and helpful as possible, be sure to disclose to your doctor exactly what you are feeling and when. Let your physician be involved in reaching conclusions about whether common speaker's nerves are the base cause of your suffering. One patient put it this way: "I have great confidence in my primary care physician. But I also recognize that he is extraordinarily busy on most days. If I begin an appointment by saying, 'Doctor, I'm experiencing speaker's nerves,' I may tilt the discussion and examination away from the real roots of my problem. So I focus on describing my symptoms, not naming my own conclusion. I let my doctor do the diagnosing."

For people already anxious about their state of nerves associated with speaking, this general advice to "see your physician" may have the unintended result of amplifying fear. My doctor? Are my symptoms a sign that I'm sick? In the great majority of cases, of course not. Your doctor's examination can actually give you confidence in narrowing the set of best solutions for your nervous discomfort; at least you leave the exam knowing what's *not* wrong.

There's also a good chance that your personal physician will be your ally in addressing the symptoms and causes of speaker's nerves. The doctor may (or may not) prescribe medication to lessen symptoms. Medications commonly used include beta-blockers to regulate heartbeat and blood pressure as well as tranquilizers such as Xanax and Ativan. Some doctors have had good luck with alternative medicines that act to calm anxiety and with lifestyle and exercise recommendations that may ease tension generally.

Just as you are experimenting with the solutions contained in this chapter, bear in mind that your physician is probably experimenting a bit to see if one or more medications or other therapies brings you relief. Too many patients feel they have somehow failed themselves and their doctor if a particular prescription brings no immediate, positive change in symptoms. If you're serious about tackling and overcoming your sensations of speaker's nerves, you must summon the courage to go back to your doctor (or another physician for another opinion, if you choose) if the first, second, or third visit doesn't yield therapeutic results for you. For most busy doctors, a patient's failure to make further contact is interpreted as a sign that the treatment worked satisfactorily. Let your doctor know what works or doesn't for you; he or she has no other way of opting for further possible modes of treatment.

Medical Treatment of Speaker's Nerves

Before tackling the treatment of your anxiety symptoms associated with public speaking, your physician will want to get all medical problems identified and properly stabilized or corrected. Because they are known to cause anxiety, several conditions should be well controlled as soon as possible. These include diabetes, hypoglycemia, thyroid disorders, heart conditions, including arrhythmias and coronary artery disease, drug or alcohol overuse, headache or other pain syndromes, autoimmune disorders such as fibromyalgia, sleep disorders, hormonal and other endocrine imbalances, and annoying digestive problems such as acid reflux and irritable bowel disorder. This treatment regimen can often be accomplished at the same time as you begin medical treatment for speech anxiety.

Also remember that other emotional conditions, especially depression, often coexist with high anxiety states. These must be recognized and treated as well. The most distressing symptoms of speaker's nerves can often be resolved with modern medications that can be prescribed by your primary care doctor or psychiatrist. Typical drugs prescribed to address the symptoms of speaker's nerves include a variety of beta-blockers such as Inderal and Toprol, which act to lower the blood pressure and prevent a racing heartbeat; benzodiazepines such as Ativan and Xanax, which calm the central nervous system; and depression-related drugs such as Prozac and Elavil, since anxiety sometimes occurs as a consequence of underlying depression. For many, these medications may well give the first real relief and sense of hope that the sufferer from speaker's nerves has felt in years. If your doctor thinks prescribed medications are indicated, don't hesitate to give them a try. Under the care of your doctor, you can always come off the medication if it isn't working or has side effects you don't like.

Although you will have a chance to talk with your doctor about your experience with speaker's nerves, doctors seldom make extensive talk therapy (in-depth and lengthy verbal counseling) a part of their own involvement with your therapy. If talk therapy is indicated, your physician will likely recommend a reputable and compatible psychologist or psychiatrist for you to see in conjunction with the physician's own treatment plan.

Working with a Mental Health Professional

The day has fortunately passed when using the services of a mental health professional stigmatized a person as "crazy." Mental issues, and the very real physical symptoms associated with them, are now viewed simply as health problems to be treated. Speaker's nerves can send you to a mental health professional as legitimately as a broken arm can send you to an orthopedist.

What can you expect on such a visit? Like your personal physician, your psychiatrist or psychologist will begin by letting you tell your whole story about speaker's nerves: how and where it began, what you feel, how you respond, and what you have tried to overcome the condition. A psychiatrist, because he or she holds a medical degree (M.D.), can prescribe drugs and will often use prescriptions in connection with talk therapy for your treatment. Typically, a series of visits lasting thirty to fifty minutes each will be scheduled over a period of weeks. During this time, your psychiatrist will monitor the effects of prescribed drugs on your condition and also pursue a course of talk therapy designed to uncover reasons for and practical solutions to your dilemma with speech anxiety.

A psychologist, who usually holds a Ph.D. instead of an M.D., will not prescribe drugs except in coordination with your physician. The bulk of time spent with a psychologist involves in-depth conversation and counseling about your feelings and attitudes. Many psychologists find that "desensitization therapy" works well for dramatically reducing the symptoms associated with speaker's nerves.

Here's how desensitization appears to work. Psychologists have long observed the "wear down" effect of the same stimuli repeated over and over. Let's take a person who suffers from fear of spiders (arachnophobia).

When this person is shown a first picture of a spider, he or she may react with revulsion and feelings of incipient panic. Those feelings may be present for the second, third, and fourth picture as well. But by the tenth or twentieth picture (especially if accompanied by reassuring language, calming music, or accompanying pleasurable imagery), the person's panicky reactions tend to dull, eventually to the point of boredom. In this case, boredom with formerly high-voltage stimuli is much to be desired.

Ideally, the fearful person will conclude from such exercises that a stimulus (the image of a spider) does not necessarily or automatically produce uncomfortable feelings—that he or she can stand such stimuli without giving in to anxious feelings. This insight by itself can be a confidence builder for sufferers from speaker's nerves and can contribute to the eventual extinguishment of their fears. Through desensitization therapy, they come to realize that the sight of a podium does not have to set their heart racing and their palms sweating.

In reality, most people with speech anxiety experience a rebound effect between desensitization sessions. In other words, they begin session two of desensitization with anxiety levels not much reduced from the levels experienced at the beginning of session one. Their habitual fearful responses, learned perhaps over a period of years of painful speaking occasions, have a perverse way of reasserting themselves and partially canceling out the progress of earlier work. But in gradual steps (two forward, one back), the emotionally freighted images of the feared experiences build up an inoculation against nervous symptoms.

As mentioned earlier in this chapter, some forms of speaker's nerves have their roots in depression, post-traumatic stress disorder, obsessive-compulsive disorder, and complicated issues of low self-worth. Although the symptoms associated with speaker's nerves can be relieved by desensitization therapies, many medical practitioners find that the sufferer's unresolved psychological problems and pressures can bring back irritating symptoms after a period of time, often in the guise of new fears and anxious obsessions. For example, a speaker who has overcome the fear of a rapid heartbeat may find him- or herself suffering a year later from recurring stomach cramps while speaking. The goal of complete therapy, therefore, is to resolve the underlying causes of speaker's nerves as well as the surface symptoms.

Summing Up

A thorough evaluative appointment with a physician includes various tests, procedures, interviews, and other diagnostic measures that may be employed in determining causes and medical solutions for the symptoms at hand. In addition, a psychiatrist (M.D.) or psychologist (Ph.D.) may apply mental health approaches to evaluate and treat the symptoms and underlying causes associated with speaker's nerves.

6

Social Phobia in Relation to
Speaker's Nerves

EARLY IN YOUR evaluation by your physician or mental health professional, the doctor will try to assess whether you suffer from social phobia. There's at least a chance, after all, that sufferers from speaker's nerves don't dislike public speaking so much as the prospect of being with other people. The issue of whether your experience with speaker's nerves indicates social phobia is not a matter of self-diagnosis. Discuss the issue with your doctor.

There are two distinct types of social phobia, also known as social anxiety disorder: generalized and nongeneralized. Generalized is the most severe form and is associated with greater impairment because the anxiety is pervasive and occurs in most, if not all, social and performance situations. The nongeneralized subtype is limited to public speaking or other performance situations. Although usually less disabling, it can still lead to significant underachievement at work or school.

Most social phobias begin before age twenty. Sufferers may describe difficulties with speaking in public, eating or drinking in a public place, participating in group meetings, using public restrooms, and meeting new people at parties or social events. People with social phobia may also fear confrontation (as, for example, in question-and-answer sessions after their speech), interaction with authority figures, and being the center of attention, as when the master of ceremonies calls on them to stand up and give a luncheon address. Fear of scrutiny by others or of being embarrassed or humiliated is described most often by people with social phobia.

The initial cause of social phobia may be a traumatic social experience. Your "most embarrassing" moment as a speaker would not have been so upsetting if the whole gang from your work division hadn't been there to witness it. Other times, the individual lacks the social skills that allow successful social interaction. A series of negative experiences and rejection over time may lead to social phobia in this case. These individuals often possess a hypersensitivity to rejection, perhaps related to dysfunction in their serotonin or dopamine neurochemical systems. Current thought points to an interaction between biological, genetic, and personality factors and environmental events.

Medical treatment and psychotherapy are useful for treating social phobia. The most widely used medications used and approved for social phobias are the serotonin-related depression drugs. Failing this, the patient may respond to a high-potency benzodiazepine, a type of tranquilizer. Beta-blockers have been used successfully for the treatment of performance anxiety on an as-needed basis. Short-acting benzodiazepines have a high potential for abuse, as does alcohol, for sufferers from speaker's nerves complicated by social phobia. But often, when people receive appropriate therapy, the medication can be tapered off gradually and eventually discontinued.

Distribution of Social Phobia in the Population

Social anxiety disorder (SAD) is the most common anxiety disorder and the third most common mental health disorder, behind major depression and alcohol dependence. The lifetime chance of getting social anxiety disorder is between 7 and 13 percent. The average age of onset is 15.5 years (Schneier et al. 1992). Many patients report being shy as young children and then becoming aware of their anxiety at the start of formal schooling. Biologically based temperamental factors during childhood, such as behavioral inhibition, may predispose some children to the development of SAD. The course of SAD is generally long, lasting an average of twenty-five years, and recovery rates are low (DeWit et al. 1999).

The reason that SAD symptoms seem to improve in older adults may be that these adults are able to afford the luxury of insulating themselves from the phobic stimuli. They may have found ways to avoid public speaking by delegating these tasks to others or by letting it be known around the office that "I don't do speeches." As senior employees, they are no longer the subject of scrutiny, as they previously were in school or the workplace. Younger adults may find a lifestyle that allows their avoidance to go unnoticed by marrying a social phobic, staying single, or choosing a job (for example, park ranger) that requires little social interaction. Although women are more likely to get the disorder, men are more likely to seek treatment. This discrepancy may be due to social expectations of society and the workplace and gender roles, with symptoms causing more impairment for men than women (Weinstock 1999). The majority of individuals with SAD are single.

The disorder has been associated with increased difficulties in school, lower educational achievement, lower socioeconomic status, more unstable employment history, and elevated rates of financial dependency. SAD has also been associated with several childhood risk factors, including parental marital conflict, frequent moves, and absence of a close, trusting relationship with an adult. SAD patients have a high rate of other coexisting psychiatric illnesses, with 81 percent reporting at least one other lifetime psychiatric diagnosis and 48 percent experiencing three other diagnoses. Over half (57 percent) admitted to having another anxiety disorder, 41 percent also had a mood disorder, and 40 percent had problems with substance abuse. Individuals with SAD frequently use alcohol to self-medicate to decrease anticipatory anxiety and reduce avoidance of feared social and/or performance situations. You have no doubt encountered an acquaintance who needed to "down a few brewskies" before a party to feel comfortable mingling with new people. Many famous stage and screen actors have fallen into the trap of needing a stiff drink (or two or three) before the curtain rises or the cameras roll. (Gardner and Bell, 2005, p. 142.)

Early Risk Factors for Social Phobia

The fears of socially phobic youth are similar to those of adults. They include fears, in social or performance situations, of being confused, blushing, doing something embarrassing, being judged stupid or weak, or having a panic attack (Essau et al. 1999). The early onset of social anxiety will likely lead to pronounced problems in adulthood. This is because of the disruptive effects of anxiety disorders on the emotionally sensitive and cognitively naive mind of a child. In addition, by the very nature of their awkward behavior, these children are more likely to have adverse social experiences that amplify their discomfort and fear. Clearly, it would be of great benefit to find ways to intervene early with this disorder as soon as it is first suspected.

Early intervention, however, requires an understanding of the disorder's precursors and risk factors. Among these factors are family genetics, temperament, parenting, information processing, social learning, and peer relationships.

The generalized subtype of SAD appears to have a stronger familial inheritance than discrete or nongeneralized social phobia. The familial risk for generalized social phobia appears to overlap with avoidant personality disorder (APD), a condition with symptoms of extreme shyness. In their study of families and social phobia, Stein and colleagues found that 74 percent of those with generalized social anxiety met the criteria for APD. Twin studies allow us to parse the relative contributions of genetic and environmental influences and estimate the heritability of the condition. In studies of 1,000 female twin pairs and 1,200 male twin pairs, Kendler and colleagues (1992–1999) were able to estimate that social phobia is inherited 50 percent of the time. It did not seem to matter whether the twins were raised apart or in the same home environment. This finding weighs against the hypothesis that social anxiety is acquired through modeling or social learning within the family. Instead, Kendler and colleagues (1999) have suggested that phobias develop when an inherited phobia proneness is activated by exposure to specific environmental stimuli. However, other studies have suggested a role for shared family environment in the development of social phobia. Lieb and colleagues (2000) found that parental anxiety and parenting style were associated with social phobia in offspring.

The fact that people with a social phobia usually have one or more other psychiatric diagnoses may also be explained by genetics. Kendler and colleagues reported evidence for an inherited "phobia proneness" with shared genetic influences on agoraphobia, social phobia, and specific phobias. This genetic liability to phobic disorders seems to overlap with that of panic disorder and bulimia. Overall, family studies have suggested that social phobia is inherited separately from panic disorder and other phobic disorders, while twin studies suggest overlapping genetic influences.

The Role of Anxious Cognitions in Speaker's Nerves

Anxious cognitions are thoughts, beliefs, and feelings resulting from the interaction of biological, social, and psychological systems. When a person with speaker's nerves fails to accurately assess these cognitions, the anxiety intensifies and is relieved only by an avoidant or defensive response. Not only do anxious thoughts themselves perpetuate the phobia, but the avoidant behaviors that follow prevent the individual from experiences that would disprove his or her fears, thereby ensuring that the phobia will persist. It has been proposed that shyness, specific social phobia, generalized social phobia, and avoidant personality disorder have similar cognitive antecedents and belong along a continuum of "concerns about social evaluation" (Rapee and Heimberg 1997). Individuals with these conditions assume that others, including audience members, are inherently critical and likely to view them negatively. At the same time, those with social anxiety attach great importance to being viewed positively by others.

It is common for socially phobic individuals to enter a social situation with a mental representation of their external appearance and behavior, as an audience might see them. Of course, they assume that this audience is looking to find fault and is prone to negative scrutiny. People with social phobia focus a great deal of attention on the internal representation of their self-image and are constantly looking for threats from the environment, such as signs of disapproval or rejection. To them, people at a party are a threatening audience rather than new friends to get to know and enjoy. It is no wonder that, with all the energy expended on searching for threatening clues and avoiding uncomfortable interaction, the social phobic's negative expectation of poor social performance is realized and reconfirmed. Cognitive therapy must be directed at correcting anxious perceptions before exposure therapy can disconfirm negative beliefs and expectations.

Conditioning Experiences and Social Phobia

Many people with speaker's nerves to the point of social phobia recall a defining embarrassing or humiliating experience associated with the onset of their disorder. In a study by Ost (1985), 58 percent of persons with social phobia could identify a traumatic social experience near or at the onset of their illness. A study by Stemberg and colleagues (1995) found that 44 percent of patients with social phobia reported a traumatic conditioning experience that started their symptoms. Most often, these experiences occurred during adolescence, a time when individuals are socially awkward and more vulnerable to embarrassment. This is also the time when most students give their first public speaking presentations—and often experience their first terrifying encounter with speaker's nerves.

It is also clear that indirect experiences can lead to conditioned fears. Ost reported that 16 percent of those with social anxiety developed their phobia by observing others undergoing traumatic social experiences, such as watching a classmate suffer through speaker's nerves, and 3 percent of his sample acquired social phobia after simply hearing about another's traumatic experience. Clearly, there must be an underlying vulnerability to anxiety to begin with, with the direct or indirect traumatic experience serving as the trigger for the development of social phobia. Temperamental factors and cognitive distortions already present may allow the trauma to be magnified and internalized. Because the condition of social phobia may have already been present before the remembered conditioning experience, it is possible that many recalled incidences represent early manifestations of the disorder rather than causal events.

Influence of Peers on Social Phobia

Peer relations in childhood appear to have significant impact on the development of social phobia and speaker's nerves. A person with anxiety and social awkwardness will likely get negative feedback in the form of peer rejection or neglect, which then exacerbates and maintains the anxiety. Children who are socially anxious generally perceive that their peer acceptance is low and report more negative interaction with peers, such as being teased or having an enemy at school (Ginsburg et al. 1998). Similarly, very shy or withdrawn children were viewed by their peers as less approachable, less socially competent, and less socially desirable (Evans 1993). These children often are the targets of victimization by schoolyard bullies. Once neglect, rejection, or victimization occurs, these experiences affect the socially anxious child's sense of self-worth. Many children with a history of peer rejection and teasing will blame themselves for having internal character deficiencies. These children experience increased loneliness, higher levels of social anxiety and avoidance, and lower self-esteem. Children who blamed their *behavior* rather than their *character* for difficulties with peers did not experience these problems (Graham and Juvonen 1998). Understanding the role of peer influences in the development of social anxiety may help educators create preventive interventions for at-risk youth.

As a case in point, Margery is a twenty-five-year-old college student with an incapacitating problem of blushing and sweating profusely in specific social situations. The phobic response was triggered by any situation where she became the center of attention. Whether it was a single person calling out her name in the grocery store to say hello or a teacher calling on her to respond to a question in front of the class, Margery would immediately feel the blood rushing to her cheeks while the sweat drenched her blouse. Her horror that others might think negatively of her (thinking her response was weak, insecure, unprepared, or stupid) prevented Margery from taking many of the participation-type classes, including the completion of speaking assignments, that were necessary for her degree in communications. She found herself falling behind in her academic program.

In Margery's initial evaluation, she disclosed that her social phobia had started at age fifteen, when her parents moved her from an all-girls high school to an all-boys school that had recently become coeducational. She was one of five girls admitted that year, and her parents were especially proud because of the new school's excellent academic standards and reputation. Margery, however, soon learned to dread going to school, where she found herself the center of all the adolescent boys' attentions. She hunched her shoulders to draw attention away from her developing breasts, which she perceived (probably correctly) to be the focus of their scrutiny. The last thing she wanted was to be stared at, so she made all attempts to avoid anything that would draw attention. The same fear of scrutiny and attention had followed her at full force into adulthood and was now threatening her academic progress.

Margery went through several sessions of cognitive-behavioral therapy, which helped reduce the anxiety in some situations. However, in performance situations in front of the class, her symptoms remained intolerable. The administration of a low-dose antidepressant (Paxil) caused sedation and made her sex life a problem (she began to have difficulty reaching orgasm). The doctor therefore tried a low-dose beta-blocker, a ten-milligram dose of propranolol, to be taken thirty minutes before the feared social situation, particularly speaking occasions. For extra assurance, the doctor also prescribed Drysol, a powerful antiperspirant, to be used on the palms of the hands and under the arms only on the morning of a presentation. Although this approach helped Margery with her difficulties at school, she still can't prevent the automatic blushing response when someone unexpectedly calls her name. For this, she will need ongoing exposure therapy to unlearn this emotional response.

Summing Up

This chapter goes into detail about social phobia, or social anxiety disorder (SAD). This discussion is not meant as a way of suggesting that all sufferers of speaker's nerves are socially phobic; rather, this is a cautionary education for readers who attach the word *just* to their symptoms: "It's just a touch of speaker's nerves"; "It's just my usual panic before presentations." A physician or mental health professional can help determine whether feelings of embarrassment, awkwardness, and isolation may indicate an underlying condition, social phobia. If so, treatment may include desensitization or cognitive-behavioral therapy (CBT).

7

Speaker's Nerves Under the Microscope

IN CHAPTER 2 we took a broad view of how the body responds in ways it believes to be appropriate to the alarm signals aroused by fears associated with public speaking. In this chapter we focus more specifically on the complex and quite wonderful electrochemistry taking place during an attack of speaker's nerves. We do so for one reason: the more you know about your body's complicated systems for responding to fear, the less you will blame yourself for specific symptoms you are feeling. You will understand that it is quite natural for cheeks to flush, palms to perspire, and heart rate to rise in response to the excitement of public speaking. Knowing what's happening in your body gives you the same sense of control and understanding experienced by a Boeing 747 pilot when the plane hits choppy air. The first-time flier worries that the plane will fall apart; the pilot reacts calmly because he or she knows why the plane is bouncing a bit. Knowledge in this case is both power and freedom.

The Physiology of Fear

We all try to avoid stressful occasions such as public speaking if they regularly trigger strong and unpleasant physical symptoms. These arise from the body's alarm system, which is designed to tell us when we are in true danger and to quickly teach us a firm, memorable lesson that will protect us in the future. In phobias and anxiety disorders, these high-intensity alarms go off when there is no true threat. The painful lessons—"don't go there," "avoid that animal," "stay away from needles," "don't volunteer for that speech," and so forth—are learned nonetheless in the emotional mind. We tend to avoid exposure to the feared object or situation thereafter, no matter how nonsensical our behavior may seem to others and even to ourselves.

One of the main problems in the development of phobias, including the fear of public speaking, is the misinterpretation of the symptom attacks caused by our anxiety alarm response. Unfortunately, many phobia symptoms, such as shortness of breath, numbness and tingling, chest pain, and dizziness, are also common in serious health events like heart attacks and strokes. Patients have every reason to seek medical care, often at emergency rooms, when these symptoms strike. Although this immediate recourse to medical evaluation is understandable, it often creates a huge expense and heavy utilization of medical services at all levels. In the real world of defensive medicine, where litigation lurks around the corner, each case must be taken seriously and worked up to rule out a true catastrophic possibility. When an anxiety attack is the diagnosis, the physician should clearly explain what happened and why. Lacking such explanations, the anxious patient will likely be back at the ER within a few weeks, seeking answers and reassurance regarding his or her symptoms.

Understanding the physiology of the fear response makes us less likely to misinterpret our symptoms, thereby preventing the development of phobic avoidance behavior and stopping our anxiety from spiraling out of control. This chapter will explain what exactly happens in your body when you experience phobic anxiety. A clear understanding of what your body is doing and why might have prevented your first bout with speaker's nerves, particularly if you were also able to control your apprehensions about what others were thinking about you at that moment.

The Mind/Body Connection

We already know intuitively that how we feel physically affects our emotions, and how we feel emotionally affects our physical sense of well-being. We are not only what we eat but also what we think, feel, and believe. In fact, the influence of mental and emotional states on physical well-being has been one of the dominant areas of medical research in recent decades. Dr. Herbert Benson of Harvard Medical School first described the "relaxation response" after studying the physiologic changes in meditating Tibetan monks. He showed how, through exercises of the mind, the monks could control such body functions as heart rate, temperature, and sweating. As lie-detector technology reveals, changes in levels of emotional stress can dramatically influence physical factors. We are now in a position to use information on the mind/body connection to carry out more successful healing strategies, including ways to overcome phobias.

Events in the Brain

Although phobic anxiety reactions may be felt in the chest and elsewhere, they begin in the brain. They affect the brain from the highest cortical centers and temporal lobes to the deeper, more primitive structures in the limbic system, basal ganglia, brain stem, and spinal cord. Once aroused by phobic alarms, the brain sends urgent electrochemical messages through the central nervous system, which, in turn, communicates with every cell and organ in the body directly or indirectly through peripheral nerves and chemical/hormonal messengers in the bloodstream. This immensely complex system of communication goes haywire if a chemical imbalance occurs in the brain, with implications for false messaging to the rest of the body. A phobic episode is often the net effect of such a chemical imbalance.

If biology class wasn't your thing, the following information on brain chemistry may seem a bit too schoolish. Nevertheless, many sufferers from speaker's nerves and other forms of phobia feel relieved when they learn that physical factors within the brain (often inherited) account for many aspects of their phobic symptoms. Imagine for a moment the unnecessary frustration in blaming pain from a broken arm on a failure of courage, personality, or character. In a similar vein, many sufferers of phobias have been blaming themselves for feelings that have a real physical cause. Therefore, I hope you will take time to at least get the basic idea of how the brain and central nervous system process alarm signals. In this section, we offer a level of detail about brain chemistry that your physician or other health professional probably cannot take the time to give you. In short, here's your chance to glimpse how it all works within the sophisticated systems of the body.

Monoamine Balance in the Brain

For four decades, the main theory to explain the biochemical basis of emotional dysfunction has been the monoamine hypothesis. According to this hypothesis, anxiety, panic, and depression result from imbalances of one or more of three biochemicals known as monoamines: serotonin, dopamine, and norepinephrine. These are the neurotransmitters that allow and facilitate communication from one neuron to the next, and from one nerve pathway to the next. When there is a prolonged deficiency in the amount of monoamine compounds, the receptors on the head of the receiving neuron become more plentiful in a process called "up-regulation." This phenomenon correlates directly with the onset of depression and anxiety. Up-regulation takes weeks to occur, and so does normalizing "down-regulation" following treatment. This explains why medical treatment takes several weeks to be effective. Popular antidepression medications (Paxil, Prozac, Zoloft, Celexa, Luvox, Lexapro) improve serotonin levels. Tricyclics increase all three monoamines. Drugs that stimulate release of monoamines from the neuron or prevent reuptake by the receiving neuron include the drugs Effexor (which acts upon serotonin and norepinephrine), Wellbutrin (dopamine and norepinephrine), and Serzone (serotonin and norepinephrine).

Serotonin Balance

Serotonin is produced in the neuron from the amino acid tryptophan. It is released into the synaptic cleft between neurons by a nerve impulse and

then destroyed by monoamine oxidase after it does its job. This brain neu-
rotransmitter is perhaps the key player in anxiety conditions. All the anxiety disorders, including obsessive-compulsive disorder (OCD), panic
disorder (PD), post-traumatic stress disorder (PTSD), and generalized anxiety disorder (GAD), have been successfully treated by medications
designed to enhance this chemical in the brain. Cell bodies of the serotonin system reside in the median and dorsal raphe nuclei of the brain
stem. Projections go to the frontal cortex (where it regulates mood), temporal lobes (triggering panic/anxiety), deep limbic and basal ganglia
(mood and anxiety conditions), hypothalamus (appetite and eating behavior), brain stem (sleep center that regulates slow-wave restorative sleep),
spinal cord (orgasm and ejaculation), and gastrointestinal system (cramps,
diarrhea, constipation, and nausea). This last connection explains why
serotonin deficiency can cause irritable bowel syndrome (IBS).

As the serotonin system is weakened by stress, the anxiety response
is more easily triggered. Deficiencies can stimulate the sympathetic (fight-
or-flight) response, while normal levels inhibit this system and promote
parasympathetic discharge (with calming effects on the nervous system).
Many conditions lead to serotonin deficiency in the brain: chronic fatigue,
chronic pain, hormonal changes, insomnia, and emotional stress. Serotonin neurons have a restraining effect on areas of the brain stem involved
in the panic response (periaqueductal gray area). The presynaptic neuron
has a reuptake pump to salvage the serotonin and pump it back into the
cell to stop neuronal communication. It is controlled by the 5HT1A presynaptic receptor. The 5HT1D presynaptic receptor blocks the release of
serotonin when stimulated, and the alpha-2 receptor blocks the release of
serotonin when norepinephrine binds to it. Drugs that inhibit these receptors allow an increase in serotonin release into the synapse and have been
found to be effective in the treatment of depression, OCD, GAD, PD,
PTSD, social phobia, drug/alcohol dependency, chronic pain, seasonal
affective disorder (SAD), and the eating disorder bulimia nervosa.

Norepinephrine Balance

The neurons of the norepinephrine system are located in the locus
ceruleus of the brain stem. These neurons make norepinephrine from the

amino acid tyrosine. Through the action of three different enzymes, tyrosine is converted first to dopamine and then to norepinephrine.

The locus ceruleus is responsible for determining whether our attention is focused on the external environment or the internal environment. Anxiety is a state where we are acutely aware of how we feel internally in our minds and bodies. There is little ability to enjoy the present moment, experiencing things outside ourselves. The locus ceruleus is the region of the mammalian brain that receives incoming information from all areas of the body, thereby monitoring the internal and external environments of the body. In turn, the locus ceruleus is wired to many areas within the brain known to be involved in the fear and anxiety response, including the amygdala (fear), limbic system, including the hippocampus and hypothalamus (emotions, energy, psychomotor retardation/agitation), frontal cortex (mood), prefrontal cortex (attention), spinal cord (sympathetic activation of bladder, heart), and cerebellum (tremors).

Hyperactivity in the norepinephrine system in the locus ceruleus is involved in the development of panic disorder. Electrical stimulation of this area in the monkey causes a fear response, while destruction reduces fear. The norepinephrine system completes its neurodevelopment by the time a person reaches the early twenties and degenerates with age. This may explain why the onset of panic disorder frequently occurs in the early twenties and seems to "burn out" as a person ages.

Dopamine Balance

Proper dopamine balance is essential for normal functioning of the basal ganglia. Attention, pleasure/reward, and motivation depend on dopamine balance.

Like norepinephrine, dopamine is synthesized in the neurons from tyrosine. It is cleaned up from the synapse by the same chemicals that remove norepinephrine from the synapse: monoamine oxidase and catechol-O-methyl transferase (COMT). Presynaptic dopamine neurons have a reuptake pump and a host of receptors, the most studied of which is the D-2 receptor. Drugs that stimulate the D-2 receptor are helpful in Parkinson's disease. Drugs that block the D-2 receptor slow down the transmission of dopamine nerve impulses, which helps schizophrenia, a disease caused by overactivity of the dopamine neurons.

Benzodiazepine/GABA Neuronal System Balance

The benzodiazepine/gamma-aminobutyric acid (GABA) neuronal system is an extensive network of linked neurons capable of modulating and suppressing neuronal excitement throughout the brain. When drugs known as benzodiazepines bind to the GABA receptors, the GABA neurons activate, thereby inhibiting anxiety and the panic response and causing muscle relaxation. The first benzodiazepine was Valium, originally invented as a muscle relaxant. Benzodiazepines are also useful in treating seizures and for the short-term treatment of insomnia. Newer hypnotic agents, including Ambien and Sonata, and the drug Gabitril bind reversibly to GABA receptors and are commonly used to treat sleep disorders.

Neurokinin Balance

The peptide neurotransmitters known as neurokinins are strings of eleven amino acids (unlike the monoamine neurotransmitters, which have one). One type of neurokinin, called substance P, has been studied in the brain and the peripheral body. In the body, it acts as a mediator of neurogenic pain, being released during times of injury and inflammation. In the brain, it seems to be responsible for our perception of pain signaled within the amygdala. This may explain why individuals with poorly controlled anxiety complain of an increase in physical pain. Drugs that block substance P appear to be able to decrease pain and anxiety in some individuals.

Melatonin and the Pineal Gland

Like serotonin, melatonin helps the nervous system adapt to a changing environment with the least amount of stress. Melatonin and serotonin inhibit the sympathetic nervous system (fight-or-flight response) and stimulate the parasympathetic system, which is associated with calming. Melatonin increases GABA, another important neurochemical in controlling anxiety. Melatonin helps us adapt to basic environmental rhythms, such as night and day. As night falls, melatonin increases and becomes a key player in signaling the start of various mental and physical restorative processes. It also accounts for much of the body's temperature rhythm, allowing the nighttime temperature drop required for sleep. Unlike serotonin, melatonin passes through the blood-brain barrier, so it can be taken directly as a supplement.

Most of the brain's melatonin is generated in the pineal gland through the conversion of serotonin. The pineal gland has a particularly elaborate blood vessel system and serves as a key modulator of the entire neurohormonal system. It is the gearshift that allows us to adapt to changing environmental conditions. Because the pineal gland is light-sensitive due to connections with the optic nerves, it allows the brain to perceive the time of day.

Melatonin deficiency has been linked to depressed mood, sleep disruption, disturbed body rhythms, agitation, increased anxiety, and higher body temperature.

Prostaglandins and Anxiety

Originally discovered in the prostate gland more than sixty years ago, prostaglandins are hormones made from only one source: essential fatty acids. Helping control the release of serotonin, prostaglandins are at the center of research in understanding depression and anxiety, as well as a wide range of general medical conditions, such as arthritis, multiple sclerosis, and even AIDS. You can get the essential fatty acids through dietary sources or supplements.

The body makes two kinds of prostaglandins, sometimes labeled "good" and "bad." In reality, both kinds are necessary for survival. The so-called good prostaglandins promote immune response, reduce inflammation (helping arthritis), inhibit cell proliferation (protecting against cancer), inhibit platelet aggregation (preventing blood clots), and promote blood vessel dilation (protecting against heart disease). The so-called bad prostaglandins balance these effects (allowing your blood to clot when it needs to, etc.).

The balance of these hormones depends on stress, age, illness, and the presence of a key essential fatty acid called eicosapentaenoic acid (EPA), which is found in high concentrations in fish oil. What we eat affects the good-to-bad ratio. Simple carbohydrates, including sugar, increase insulin, which promotes the bad prostaglandins. Good (PGE1) prostaglandin has been shown to be associated with an elevated mood (thought to cause the initial elation of alcohol). Bad (PGE2) prostaglandin increases with anxiety, anger, or hostility.

The Deep Limbic System

The deep limbic system is at the center of the brain. Only about the size of a walnut, it is critical for human emotion and behavior. It is an "older" part of the mammalian brain, setting the mammals apart from the reptiles, which behave in a more predictable way dictated by the brain stem. This is why a dog is apparently more emotional than an alligator. The dog forms limbic bonds through physical contact such as licking and smelling. Human beings also store emotional memories, such as the smell of something (or someone) we love, the taste of a food we are passionate about, a voice we trust (or fear), and so forth. The deep limbic system adds the emotional desire, passion, and drive to our organizational, problem-solving, and rational cerebral cortex. It is in this part of the brain that our phobic emotional memories are stored and triggered when we are confronted by the phobic stimulus.

When the deep limbic system is quiet and calm, the person's state of mind is generally positive and hopeful. When the system is overactive and heated up, negativity takes over. Hyperactivity in the deep limbic system directly correlates with negative emotions. This was demonstrated consistently in SPECT scan studies by Daniel Amen, M.D. (SPECT stands for *single photon emission computerized tomography*, a nuclear medicine study that "looks" directly at cerebral blood flow and indirectly at brain activity through level of metabolism.) The deep limbic system sets the emotional tone of the body, stores emotional memories, promotes bonding, modulates libido, processes sense of smell, controls appetite and sleep, tags events as internally important, and sets the emotional tone of the mind. Problems in this system cause moodiness, irritability, depression, negative thinking, negative perspective, appetite and sleep problems, social isolation, decreased or increased sexual responsiveness, and problems with motivation ("I just don't care").

Women, on average, have larger limbic systems than men. This fact gives women the advantage of being more expressive of their emotions and more in touch with them. Typically, women are better able to bond and connect with others, helping to explain why they are the primary caretakers of children in all societies on earth. Men are more likely to be disconnected from others, due to less limbic bonding. But women are also more susceptible to depression, especially at times of hormonal changes. Women attempt suicide three times more often than men, although men are three times more successful because they use more violent means.

The deep limbic area is "wired" by nerve connections directly to the prefrontal cortex, the supervisory part of the brain, which takes up to about age twenty-one to develop fully. When the deep limbic system is activated, emotions take control, while the more rational prefrontal cortex is inhibited. Often, the more emotional you become, the less rational and "in control" you are.

Amygdala and Basal Ganglia

The amygdala and basal ganglia deserve special mention, because they play a central role in anxiety. The central nucleus of the amygdala is where learning processes relevant to fear and anxiety occur. In turn, its neurons are strongly interconnected with the hypothalamus and the brain stem regions, which are responsible for triggering the physical symptoms of anxiety and panic. When the amygdala neurochemical N-methyl-D-aspartate (NMDA) is blocked, the acquisition of conditioned fear responses also is blocked.

The basal ganglia are a set of large structures toward the center of the brain, surrounding the deep limbic system. They are involved in the integration of feelings, thoughts, and movement. They set the body's "idle speed" or anxiety level. The functioning of this area of the brain accounts for why you jump when you're excited, tremble when you're nervous, or get tongue-tied when you're angry. It decides how easily you startle. If there is too much input, as in an accident or other stressful situation, they tend to "lock up." People who already have overactive basal ganglia due to an anxiety disorder are more likely to be overwhelmed by stressful situations, freezing up in action and thought. Underactive basal ganglia have been associated with attention deficit disorder (ADD). In this case, the stressful situation moves them to action. People with ADD are often able to react to a stressful situation without fear, and they are frequently the first on the scene of an accident. Underactive basal ganglia are associated with low motivation and energy, while overactivity causes anxiety, tension, increased awareness, and heightened fear. Many highly motivated individuals show increased activity in this area, which may be the key to their success. The drug Ritalin increases dopamine release in the basal ganglia, helping motivation, mental focus, and follow-through. Cocaine powerfully increases dopamine in the basal ganglia, and, interestingly, so does love.

Problems in the basal ganglia are implicated in anxiety, panic, physical symptoms of anxiety (heart pounding, difficulty breathing, nausea, sweating, hot or cold flashes, dizziness, feeling faint, tension headaches, sore muscles, hand tremor), low threshold of embarrassment, quick startle reaction, tendency to predict the worst, worry about what others think, fear of dying or doing something crazy, feeling off-balanced, shyness and timidity, pessimism, conflict avoidance, Tourette's syndrome (motor and vocal tics), muscle tension and soreness, tremors, fine-motor problems, headaches, and low or excessive motivation. Tourette's syndrome involves involuntary physical movements and noises such as coughing, puffing, blowing, barking, and sometimes swearing (coprolalia). It can be inherited through several genetic abnormalities found in the dopamine family of genes. Among those with Tourette's syndrome, 60 percent have ADD, and 50 percent have OCD. All of these conditions seem to have a similar connection through dysfunction in the basal ganglia. (Gardner and Bell, 2005, p. 153.)

Cognitive-behavioral therapy (CBT) and guided imagery are especially helpful for quieting overactive basal ganglia. So are deep breathing, meditation, and self-hypnosis. Anger and stress management also offer important techniques that help quiet the basal ganglia.

Emotional Molecules

Medical schools in the mid-1980s taught that the nervous system and the immune system operate relatively independently of one another. We have since discovered that nerves connect the immune system to the nervous system, which is directly wired to the brain. We have also found a host of neuropeptides, molecules that carry messages between the brain and every cell in the body, enabling them to be in constant communication with one another. The brain and endocrine system are also in constant communication through direct nerve channels and bloodstream-borne chemical messengers.

The somatic dysfunctions caused by anxiety attacks can be explained fully by the interconnection of the mind and body through the nervous system and chemical messengers. During the fight-or-flight response, the mind, under the influence of fear, sends neurological and chemical signals to the endocrine glands, heart, gut, muscles, and blood vessels to react in predictable ways. These signals alter, redirect, and disrupt the body's normal regulatory functions, causing a myriad of symptoms.

EEG, PET, and SPECT Scan Studies

Electroencephalogram (EEG) studies have shown that panic disorder is linked to an inherited trait of low-voltage alpha waves (the brain waves involved in the relaxation response). Alcoholics with anxiety are ten times more likely than a normal control group to have low-voltage alpha waves. Depression patients exhibit a reduction in alpha wave (REM) sleep time. Neuroimaging techniques (PET and SPECT scans) show differences in brain structure, circulation, and metabolism between those with emotional illness and normal controls. These studies have shown that frontal, temporal, and limbic/hippocampal areas are activated in patients with panic disorder. The amygdalocortical pathway is activated during fear conditioning. Depressed patients show activation of the deep limbic system.

Sympathetic and Parasympathetic Nervous Systems

Fear can originate in the conscious, highly developed cortex of the brain or in the deeper, more primitive centers that control our emotional and subconscious awareness. In either case, the signals of fear reach the hypothalamus gland. The hypothalamus, in the seat of the deep limbic system, is a crucial brain structure in understanding the mind/body connection. It translates our emotional state into physical feelings of relaxation or tension. The front half of the hypothalamus sends calming signals to the body through the parasympathetic nervous system, while the back half sends stimulating fear signals via the sympathetic nervous system. It is the sympathetic system that triggers the fight-or-flight response when a person faces a threat. A combination of parasympathetic inhibition decreasing vagus nerve input and increasing sympathetic activation causes increased heart rate, breathing rate, and blood pressure. The hands and feet go cool, and the pupils dilate (presumably so the person can see better).

The hypothalamus also makes control hormones that tell the pituitary gland which endocrine glands it should activate. At the time of stress, it causes the pituitary to release a chemical, which circulates through the bloodstream to the adrenal gland, causing the release of "stress hormones," including adrenaline, noradrenaline, and cortisol from the adrenal glands. These hormones bind to receptor sites on cells and can activate a variety of responses and symptoms, such as tremors, sweats, more forceful heartbeat, diarrhea, nausea, and hyperventilation with lightheadedness. Beta-blockers are drugs that block the beta receptors where these hormones attach, thereby stopping these unpleasant symptoms.

Hypothalamic triggering of the sympathetic nervous system activates a cascade of hormonal and neurological messages that flow throughout the body. These exert an effect on many different organs and systems, as well as on the person's behavior:

- **Cardiovascular system.** The heart rate increases, and the amount of blood pumped out with each beat (stroke volume) increases. These factors result in an increase in the blood pressure to improve circulation.

Blood flow also is redirected as involuntary smooth muscles that surround our arteries are stimulated to either relax or constrict. Relaxation causes the artery to open up and allow more blood flow to the most vital tissues. Constriction cuts back the circulation to less important areas. During the fight-or-flight response, the blood carries the necessary nutrients, especially oxygen and sugar, faster and in larger amounts to the big muscles of the arms and legs, the heart, lungs, and brain. In contrast, blood flow decreases to the skin, hands, feet, kidneys, and digestive system. You may notice that your hands and feet go numb, tingle, or feel cold during anxiety attacks, due to this aspect of sympathetic nervous system activation. Additionally, the blood coagulates faster to protect against excessive blood loss in case of injury. This combination of higher blood pressure and faster coagulation may make some individuals more vulnerable to a stroke or heart attack during a period of anxiety. The symptoms of a heart attack are common, with 35 percent of those who experience anxiety complaining of chest pain and heart palpitations (fast or irregular heart rhythm).

■ **Pulmonary system.** Breathing becomes deeper and faster to supply more oxygen to the larger muscles that may be asked to fight or run. As we hyperventilate, we not only get more oxygen into the blood, but we also blow off the carbon dioxide as we exhale, reducing the blood concentration of this gas. This imbalance in blood gases can also lead to dizziness, nausea, and numbness and tingling in the arms and legs.

■ **Sweat glands.** The sympathetic nervous system stimulates increased sweating, which helps the body regulate its temperature. Some patients describe this phenomenon as "breaking out in a cold sweat."

■ **Central nervous system.** The mind goes on high alert, as all senses become heightened and we are capable of focusing intensely on the present danger (or, in phobic situations, what we erroneously perceive as the present danger). This full alert can be seen on the brain wave machine, or electroencephalogram, as a rapid firing of beta brain waves. Emotions of anger and/or fear arise from the basal ganglia and amygdala centers deep in the brain. At this point, we may experience an overwhelming sense of doom. Many people having an anxiety attack for the first time, especially if the attack is severe, truly feel they are dying.

- **Behavior.** When a phobia causes activation of the sympathetic nervous system, we will usually either fight or flee. Imagine someone with a phobia to bees. One lone honeybee may set off an angry and aggressive flurry of flailing arms and legs in an attempt to kill the creature, or the phobic behavior might motivate a person to jump into the nearest body of water. The reaction of paralysis also is possible when the fear is so powerful that the person cannot move, scream, or react. He or she will often say of the experience, "I was so scared that I couldn't move or speak. I was paralyzed with fear."

Reversing all these physiological events requires the functioning of the parasympathetic nervous system. The heart rate is slowed down through parasympathetic vagus nerve stimulation, which also reduces stroke volume and blood pressure. Blood flow returns to the hands and feet as smooth muscles in the peripheral arteries begin to relax. Breathing slows, restoring a normal balance of oxygen and carbon dioxide in the blood, and sweating subsides as the body's temperature drops back down to normal. In the mind, beta brain waves decrease as alpha brain waves amplify.

Summing Up

That's the short course in complex physiologies associated with speaker's nerves and other phobias. Standing in awe of the interconnected systems active during fear responses, including speaker's nerves, can in itself lead to a calming thought: the brain is an amazing control center that is well equipped to keep the body functioning normally—if we prevent fearful thoughts from interfering.

This chapter mines more deeply into brain and body functions involved in the fear response and the parasympathetic normalizing that takes place afterward. Learning details about specific electrochemical pathways and interactions is one way you can equip yourself with background understanding of the physiology of fear. If a physician or psychiatrist prescribes a medication to relieve symptoms of speaker's nerves, the specific information included in this chapter can help you understand what you are taking, how it is intended to alter or regulate particular parts of the brain or body, and what long-term results you can expect.

Appendix A

A Planning Guide for Overcoming Speaker's Nerves

THE FOLLOWING WORKSHEETS can be helpful in several ways. First, you have an opportunity to write out the full story of your battle with speaker's nerves, so you can see it whole, rather than in the fragments of various occurrences over months or years. Second, your completed pages provide a description of symptoms you can share with a friend or with your physician or mental health professional. Finally, the worksheets give you a planning guide for specifying recovery goals, selecting solutions, and tracking progress.

Suggestions: Fill out the worksheets as spontaneously as possible, writing more for yourself than for anyone else. Turn back to the chapters in this book to review lists of symptoms, making sure you have not skipped any that you experience. In your entries, try to be as descriptive as possible, telling what you felt ("an irregular thumping in my upper chest and throat"), instead of giving only terms and conclusions ("heart palpitations").

I. Your History with Speaker's Nerves

When did you first experience speaker's nerves?

Approximate date: _____

Approximate time: _____

Place: _____

Situation (what you were doing): _____

On this first encounter with speaker's nerves, what did you experience? (Review the symptoms in Chapters 1 and 2, and then jot down the full list of what you felt, whether or not these symptoms appear in the book.)

_____

_____

_____

_____

_____

_____

Looking back, why do you think you experienced speaker's nerves on this first occasion?

_____

_____

_____

_____

_____

_____

_____

Have speaker's nerves recurred since this first experience?

_____

_____

If yes, provide the following information:

How often?

_____

In what situations?

_____

Can you predict when speaker's nerves will occur? Explain.

_____

_____

_____

_____

Do symptoms vary in type from one experience to another? Explain.

_____

_____

_____

_____

What symptoms bother you most in these experiences?

_____

_____

_____

_____

Are symptoms getting worse, getting better, or staying the same? Explain.

_____

_____

_____

_____

If you have not experienced another episode of speaker's nerves, why do you believe you haven't?

_____

_____

_____

_____

Do you worry that speaker's nerves will occur again? Discuss your feelings.

_____

_____

_____

_____

_____

How has speaker's nerves affected your professional/work life? Be specific.

_____

_____

_____

_____

_____

_____

How has speaker's nerves affected your personal life? Be specific.

_____

_____

_____

_____

_____

II. Your Symptoms of Speaker's Nerves

Your Symptoms List

Write down each of the symptoms you feel during an episode of speaker's nerves. For each symptom, specify "always," "frequently," "sometimes," or "rarely" to tell how often a particular symptom is a part of your experience of speaker's nerves.

Symptom: EXAMPLE: breathlessness

Description of what this symptom feels like:

EXAMPLE: I feel as if I can't catch my breath, even my breathing is fast. My upper chest feels tight.

Symptom: _____

Description of what this symptom feels like:

_____

_____

_____

_____

_____

Symptom: _____

Description of what this symptom feels like:

_____

_____

_____

_____

_____

_____

Symptom: _____

Description of what this symptom feels like:

_____

_____

_____

_____

_____

_____

Symptom: _____

Description of what this symptom feels like:

_____

_____

_____

_____

_____

_____

Symptom: _____

Description of what this symptom feels like:

_____
_____
_____
_____
_____

Symptom: _____

Description of what this symptom feels like:

_____
_____
_____
_____
_____

Onset of Your Symptoms

What do you feel at the very beginning of an encounter with speaker's nerves?

_____
_____
_____

What do you feel next?

_____
_____
_____

What do you experience at the "high point" or worst part of speaker's nerves?

_____

_____

_____

_____

How long do symptoms last? Be specific for each symptom.

_____

_____

_____

_____

How can you tell when speaker's nerves are subsiding?

_____

_____

_____

_____

How do you feel immediately after symptoms have disappeared?

_____

_____

_____

How do you feel a few hours after symptoms have disappeared?

_____

_____

_____

Severity of Symptoms

Which symptoms bother or frighten you most during an episode of speaker's nerves?

Symptom: _____

Symptom: _____

Symptom: _____

Symptom: _____

Tell about one of your typical episodes of speaker's nerves.

_____

_____

_____

_____

_____

_____

_____

_____

Tell about your worst experience with speaker's nerves.

_____

_____

_____

_____

_____

_____

_____

III. Your Goals

In answering the following questions, assume that you cannot snap your fingers and make speaker's nerves disappear immediately. What goal would you like to achieve right away with regard to episodes of speaker's nerves?

_____

_____

_____

Once that goal is met, what goals would you like to achieve next? List as many as you wish, in order of importance to you.

Goal: _____

_____

_____

Goal: _____

_____

_____

Goal: _____

_____

_____

Goal: _____

_____

_____

How will your professional/work life be different if you meet your goals?

_____

_____

_____

_____

_____

_____

_____

_____

How will your personal life be different if you meet your goals?

_____

_____

_____

_____

_____

_____

_____

_____

_____

IV. Your Options

Tell about any medical or psychological evaluation you have received with regard to your experience of speaker's nerves.

_____

_____

_____

_____

_____

If you have not discussed your speaker's nerves with your physician and/or mental health professional, do you want to? Explain your feelings.

_____

_____

_____

_____

Why do you think you experience speaker's nerves? Discuss any aspect of your life (work responsibilities, home life, relationships, pressures, habits, health issues, personality, heredity, and so forth) that you feel may play a role in causing your speaker's nerves.

_____

_____

_____

_____

_____

_____

_____

After reviewing the lists of suggested remedies for speaker's nerves in Chapters 4 and 5 answer the following questions. Which solution(s) do you believe is most likely to relieve your speaker's nerves? Explain why.

_____

_____

_____

_____

_____

When will you try out this possible solution? Be specific about the time, place, and situation.

_____

_____

_____

_____

_____

_____

How will you decide if your chosen solution(s) is achieving the result you seek?

_____

_____

_____

_____

_____

_____

If you have to turn to other solutions, which do you want to try?

Solution: _____

Solution: _____

Solution: _____

Why?

_____

_____

_____

_____

V. Your Plan and Time Line

Write down a calendar of specific action steps you plan to take to resolve your problems with speaker's nerves. For example, if you plan to see a doctor and/or mental health professional for an evaluation of your symptoms, write down when that visit will occur. If you plan to try out one or more solutions for speaker's nerves at an upcoming speaking event, tell when that event will occur and what solutions you will try. In your calendar, try to plan ahead for at least the next thirty days.

_____

_____

_____

_____

_____

_____

_____

_____

_____

_____

_____

_____

_____

_____

VI. Your Support System

Name the individuals (preserve confidentiality, if you wish) with whom you have discussed your problems with speaker's nerves.

_____

_____

_____

_____

_____

_____

_____

_____

In what ways have these people helped you so far in overcoming speaker's nerves? How do you want them to help you in the future? Be specific.

_____

_____

_____

_____

_____

_____

_____

_____

_____

Your Progress So Far (based on your time line in Section VII).

If you have already met with your physician and/or mental health professional for an evaluation of your symptoms, what was the outcome of that visit? (Tell what your doctor found and what he or she recommended. Specify any treatment or prescription.)

_____

_____

_____

_____

_____

If you have met with your physician and/or mental health professional, tell how you feel about the results of that visit. For example, are you satisfied with the doctor's evaluation and recommendations? Is the doctor working for you? Specify any unanswered questions or remaining problems you want to address with your doctor.

_____

_____

_____

_____

_____

Which solution(s), if any, appears to be working in resolving your problems with speaker's nerves? Describe any progress you have made.

_____

_____

_____

_____

_____

_____

If you feel you have not made significant progress in resolving speaker's nerves, try to explain why the solution(s) you have chosen has not worked to your satisfaction.

_____

_____

_____

_____

_____

If the route back from speaker's nerves to confident presenting is 100 miles long, at which mile marker do you believe you have arrived? Specifically what will you do to complete your journey to confident speaking?

_____

_____

_____

_____

_____

_____

_____

_____

_____

_____

_____

_____

_____

_____

_____

_____

_____

_____

_____

_____

Appendix B

Evaluating Your Personality Characteristics with the
Speaker's Personality Instrument (SPI)

SEVERAL CHAPTERS IN this book have provided options for discovering why
you experience speaker's nerves. This appendix offers one more possibility: your approach to public speaking may be running counter to strong
preferences and habits within your personality. The Speaker's Personality
Instrument, the short evaluation in this appendix, will help you determine
aspects of your personality that may shed light on why you experience
speaker's nerves at one time but not another, in one location but not
another, and with one group of listeners but not another.

Here's how the instrument works. For each pair of answer choices
provided per question, select the one choice that you prefer over the other
choice. (If you don't agree completely with either choice, choose the one
that you agree with more.) Follow the scoring guide at the end of the
instrument to arrive at numerical scores in eight areas:

- Member
- Self
- Juggler
- Planner
- Thinker
- Empathizer
- Closer
- Researcher

Your highest scores among these categories indicate dominant aspects of your personality. Use the score interpretation information at the end of the appendix to understand more fully how aspects of your personality may be implicated in your experience of speaker's nerves—and what to do to address the problem.

Here's a bit of historical context for the Speaker's Personality Instrument. It is based on the psychological theories of Swiss philosopher Carl Jung, which continue to provide an influential tool for understanding interpersonal relations, including anxiety conditions that occur within and among individuals. In 1921, Jung proposed the "type" theory—the idea that each of us is predisposed to certain personality tendencies, which Jung arranged into four dimensions, each composed of opposite qualities. Some individuals, Jung said, are by nature more extroverted, some are more introverted. Some spend their energy handling details, while others work to grasp the big picture. Some operate predominantly by logic, some by emotion. Some are data gatherers, while others hurry on to conclusions.

Knowing "who you are" in this scheme of personality definition can help you predict and prepare for personalities quite unlike yours (in other words, people with whom you may experience conflict and verbal sparring).

Here's how this evaluation works. You simply enter your "a" or "b" choices on the scorecard following the questions. The interpretive guide accompanying the scorecard will help you understand your scores and make applications to your business life.

Speaker's Personality Instrument (SPI)

Directions

Read each question and choose one of the possible responses, allowing your gut response to guide your choice. In some cases, you may not have a strong preference, or neither of the answers may seem to be right for you. In all cases, choose the answer that comes closer to your opinion. (It may be most convenient to circle "a" or "b" for each question, and then transfer your answers to the scorecard when you have completed the test.)

1. In the workplace, do you prefer
   - (a) making social conversation with many people during the day?
   - (b) making social conversation with only a few people during the day?

2. In learning a new work skill, do you prefer to be trained by
   - (a) following a step-by-step set of instructions?
   - (b) grasping the big picture and trying your own approach?

3. Do your work associates value you most for
   - (a) what you think (that is, your rational abilities)?
   - (b) what you feel (your "heart" or intuitions)?

4. As you review major accomplishments by others in your industry, do you believe their achievements have been due to
   - (a) pushing hard to make things happen?
   - (b) looking beyond obvious answers for new possibilities?

5. In your work relationships, do you consider yourself
   - (a) popular with many people?
   - (b) popular with only a few people?

6. In considering a job change, would you prefer to hear about
   - (a) what employees at a new company are doing?
   - (b) how employees at the new company are being prepared for future challenges?

7. When a new worker enters your work environment, do you form impressions based on
   (a) his/he/him appearance and actions?
   (b) the way they make you feel when you are with them?

8. In making business purchases, do you select items
   (a) quickly, because you know what you want?
   (b) after careful comparison shopping?

9. At work do you prefer jobs that
   (a) bring you in contact with many people during the day?
   (b) bring you in contact with few if any people during the day?

10. When you have too much to do in your day, do you respond by
    (a) finding extra energy to meet the challenges?
    (b) stopping to revise your plans and schedules?

11. In managing others, would it be more important for you to be
    (a) logical?
    (b) friendly?

12. In arranging business deals, would you tend to
    (a) save time for all concerned by spelling out the major points of agreement and leaving minor points to good faith between the parties?
    (b) spell out both major and minor details, even if such work takes extra time?

13. At work do you consider yourself to have
    (a) many friends?
    (b) few if any friends?

14. Do you think a company leader should be
    (a) informative?
    (b) organized?

15. When a coworker confides in you about a personal problem, do you tend at first to
    (a) try to offer a possible solution?
    (b) feel and express sympathy?

16. In superior-subordinate relationships at work, should duties between the parties be
    (a) stated clearly in written or spoken form?
    (b) left open to allow for flexibility and new opportunities?

17. When meeting a new employee, do you tend to
    (a) take the initiative in showing warmth and friendliness?
    (b) wait for him or her to show signs of friendliness?

18. Should children be raised to
    (a) learn real-world skills and behaviors as soon as they are ready?
    (b) set goals and stick to their commitments?

19. In work relationships, is it more dangerous to show
    (a) too much emotion and personality?
    (b) too little emotion and personality?

20. In designing interview questions for use in hiring a manager, would you tend to create
    (a) questions with definite answers?
    (b) questions that are open-ended?

21. An old acquaintance (but not a good friend) unexpectedly encounters you in the lobby of a convention hotel. Do you tend to find this chance meeting
    (a) enjoyable?
    (b) somewhat uncomfortable?

22. In choosing artwork to hang on company walls, would you tend to choose paintings that
    (a) are quite different from one another?
    (b) work together to communicate a single theme or impression?

23. In deciding which candidate to support for a leadership position in your company, would you favor
    (a) an intelligent, coolheaded candidate?
    (b) a passionate and well-intentioned candidate?

24. Do you prefer social get-togethers that are
    (a) carefully planned?
    (b) largely unplanned?

25. In going out to lunch with coworkers, would you prefer to be with
    (a) many coworkers?
    (b) one or two coworkers?

26. Presidents of companies should have
    (a) excellent skills.
    (b) well-developed plans.

27. You are passing through a city on business and want to stop to say hello to a former colleague who lives there. Would you prefer to
    (a) make specific time and place arrangements with the person well in advance of your trip?
    (b) give the person a pleasant surprise by a call "out of the blue"?

28. When attending a company social event taking place at 8:00 P.M., do you tend to
    (a) arrive right on time?
    (b) arrive somewhat late?

29. In making business phone calls, do you
    (a) make most of the conversation, allowing little time for the other person to speak?
    (b) spend most of your time listening and commenting briefly on what the other person is saying?

30. In moments of leisure, would you prefer to read
    (a) a letter to the editor in a newsmagazine?
    (b) an article about city planning?

31. In choosing movies, do you tend to select
    (a) movies that explain social conditions and historical periods?
    (b) movies that produce laughter or tears?

32. In preparing to be interviewed for a job, do you think you should prepare to talk more about
    (a) your achievements?
    (b) your future goals and plans?

33. If forced to accept dormitory accommodations during a conference, would you prefer to stay in a room
    (a) with a few other compatible conference participants?
    (b) alone?

34. In making work decisions, are you most influenced by
    (a) the facts of the situation at hand?
    (b) the implications of the situation at hand?

35. If you are hiring employees to work for you, should they be primarily
    (a) intelligent and wise?
    (b) loyal and hardworking?

36. In purchasing real estate, is it more important to
    (a) be ready to snap up a good deal before it disappears?
    (b) have thorough knowledge of available properties?

37. In making a consumer complaint, would you prefer to
    (a) call the company and talk to a customer representative?
    (b) write to the company?

38. When performing an ordinary work task, do you prefer to
    (a) do whatever works?
    (b) do what is usually done?

39. In court, judges should
    (a) follow the letter of the law.
    (b) show leniency or strictness where they think it appropriate.

40. When given a project to complete, would you prefer that someone give you
    (a) a deadline?
    (b) the freedom to turn in the project when you feel it is ready?

41. When introducing two work associates who do not know each other, do you tend to
    (a) tell them each a bit of information about the other to facilitate conversation?
    (b) let them make their own conversation?

42. Which is worse for a manager?
    (a) to be too idealistic
    (b) to be too flexible

43. When you listen to a business presentation, do you prefer a speaker
    (a) who proves his or her points with data and specific examples?
    (b) who communicates excitement and deep commitment to the topic?

44. At the end of the workday, do you spend more time thinking about
    (a) what you did during the day?
    (b) what you are going to do the next day?

45. In planning your ideal vacation, would you choose a place where
    (a) you can meet with family and friends?
    (b) you can be alone or with only one or two family members or friends?

46. At work, which activity appeals to you more?
    (a) meeting deadlines
    (b) predicting coming events

47. Which would be more important to you if you were president of a company?
    (a) that all employees understand their job responsibilities thoroughly
    (b) that all employees feel part of the company family

48. As a member of a project team, would you prefer to be most involved in
    (a) the completion stage in which final details are wrapped up?
    (b) the initial conceptualization stage in which approaches are debated?

49. In learning a new work skill, would you prefer to be taught
    (a) as part of a small class?
    (b) one-on-one by a trainer?

50. If you had just two novels to choose between for leisure reading, would you be more likely to select
    (a) a realistic novel about people and places?
    (b) a mystery novel at the end of which everything becomes clear?

51. When you consider your career path, do you believe you should
    (a) plan career moves months or years in advance?
    (b) follow your heart as opportunities arise?

52. In paying tribute to a retiring company leader, should you focus primarily on
    (a) the person's achievements?
    (b) the person's aspirations?

53. Do you think the main purpose of meetings in business is
    (a) getting to know one another and building team spirit?
    (b) getting work done as efficiently as possible?

54. Are you more adept at
    (a) drawing conclusions from facts?
    (b) raising long-term questions and issues?

55. The most important quality that a workforce can have is
    (a) up-to-date education.
    (b) team spirit.

56. Which of the following words comes closest to describing your behavior at work?
    (a) impatient
    (b) curious

57. If your employer wanted to honor you at a luncheon, would you prefer a luncheon attended by
    (a) many company employees?
    (b) your employer and one or two others?

58. In general, which quality has mattered more for highly successful companies?
    (a) common sense
    (b) foresight

59. If you had to choose, which of these two things would be better to say about a retiring employee?
    (a) that he or she was smart at his or her job
    (b) that he or she cared deeply about coworkers

60. In working on a team project, do you tend to
    (a) move it along to completion before the due date?
    (b) make sure team members have considered all relevant information?

Scorecard

Transfer your answers as checks in the appropriate spaces below.

1a __	1b __	2a __	2b __	3a __	3b __	4a __	4b __
5a __	5b __	6a __	6b __	7a __	7b __	8a __	8b __
9a __	9b __	10a __	10b __	11a __	11b __	12a __	12b __
13a __	13b __	14a __	14b __	15a __	15b __	16a __	16b __
17a __	17b __	18a __	18b __	19a __	19b __	20a __	20b __
21a __	21b __	22a __	22b __	23a __	23b __	24a __	24b __
25a __	25b __	26a __	26b __	27a __	27b __	28a __	28b __
29a __	29b __	30a __	30b __	31a __	31b __	32a __	32b __
33a __	33b __	34a __	34b __	35a __	35b __	36a __	36b __
37a __	37b __	38a __	38b __	39a __	39b __	40a __	40b __
41a __	41b __	42a __	42b __	43a __	43b __	44a __	44b __
45a __	45b __	46a __	46b __	47a __	47b __	48a __	48b __
49a __	49b __	50a __	50b __	51a __	51b __	52a __	52b __
53a __	53b __	54a __	54b __	55a __	55b __	56a __	56b __
57a __	57b __	58a __	58b __	59a __	59b __	60a __	60b __

TOTAL: M ___ S ___ J ___ P ___ T ___ E ___ C ___ R ___

Add up the total number of checks in each column. Then for each pair of letters at the bottom of the columns, circle the letter for the column containing more checks. You should circle four letters in total. The letters refer to the eight personality descriptions presented, from which you will be highlighting four. The greater the number of checks, the more dominant that characteristic is in your personality.

Why four dominant traits? None of us consistently acts in accordance with only one personality characteristic. Instead, various traits (such as those you've identified by the letters you've circled) interact, often in unpredictable ways, to produce the whole personality known as "you."

Let's say, for example, that your score identifies you as MJEC, meaning you have dominant traits in the Member, Juggler, Empathizer, and Closer categories. Read through the descriptions of these personality types, and reflect on how those traits interact in your personality. Perhaps in times of stress, one or more traits come to the fore. Perhaps some traits are more evident at home, while others are dominant at work.

Personality Characteristics

M—Member

Individuals with a Member personality are predisposed to enjoy and seek out the company of others. The Member joins groups willingly, finds ways to include others in activities, and may tend to avoid tasks that must be accomplished alone. The Member relies on the consensus of the group for important decisions and may hesitate to form or express personal opinions without having them validated first by the group. The Member derives emotional support and strength from belonging, popularity, and the respect of others.

Members tend to experience speaker's nerves when they are left guessing how others feel about their presentation. This problem can occur during one-way presentations out of the view of an audience, as in the case of a podcast, videotaped speech, or teleconference. In those situations, because the Member doesn't know whether listeners like or dislike what they have seen and heard, he or she feels anxious. Members can also experience speaker's nerves when they speak before an audience they don't know. For a Member, being "odd person out" in a social environment where all the others appear to know one another can be disconcerting to the point of speaker's nerves.

One solution to the risk of speaker's nerves is for the Member to get to know several audience members, however briefly, before speaking to a group of strangers. In the case of electronic one-way presentations, the Member can use e-mail surveys to get feedback from those who watched and heard the broadcast.

S—Self

Someone with a Self personality is predisposed to individual initiation and solitary work habits. The Self joins a group only for a compelling reason, and even then only for the period of the task at hand. The Self looks with suspicion on widely held opinions and groupthink. When faced with tasks too extensive or difficult for a single person to accomplish, the Self opts to divide work tasks into portions that can each be managed by an individual. The Self derives emotional support and strength from measuring up to personal standards, not the judgment of others.

The Self tends to experience speaker's nerves when he or she feels social pressure to say and do things against his or her better judgment. This type of person may feel uncomfortable jitters if selected by team members to express their point of view but not his or her own. Making a presentation as part of a panel can rattle the Self, who may feel that his or her individual opinion is being overshadowed by the dominant voices on the panel.

One solution for the Self is to prepare a thorough handout—a "white paper" of sorts—that fully expresses his or her point of view. The Self can then relax somewhat when facing social pressure, knowing that his or her core message will still get out to audience members via the handout.

J—Juggler

A person with a Juggler personality is predisposed to make minute-by-minute, seemingly practical adjustments to changing conditions. The Juggler manages to keep many tasks in progress at once, all in a partial state of completion. The panic of impending deadlines and the unpredictability of interruptions and emergencies are energizing and challenging for the Juggler. It is a matter of pride to the Juggler that he or she can handle situations, cope, and eventually see projects through to fulfillment. The Juggler derives emotional support and strength from a sense of sustained busyness as well as a conviction that he or she is special and valuable to the group.

Jugglers may experience speaker's nerves if forced to prepare for a presentation in what they perceive to be a plodding, step-by-step way. Jugglers want to "get this show on the road" and claim they are ready to speak "right now." Yielding to the methods and schedules of other personality types can be excruciatingly irritating to a Juggler. These feelings may express themselves eventually as speaker's nerves when it comes time to give the presentation, especially if the Juggler has ended up in hostile relations with other team members.

One solution to the Juggler's risk of speaker's nerves is to multitask—as politely as possible—while others twiddle their coffee spoons in endless, seemingly pointless meetings (at least from the Juggler's point of view). Jugglers can feel more relaxed about their presenting responsibilities if they find ways to busy themselves during the development process.

P—Planner

An individual with a Planner personality is predisposed to place details, individual facts, and other data into patterns. The Planner then clings to these patterns tenaciously, for they serve to organize an otherwise bewildering array of discrete items. The Planner resists receiving disorganized data before a plan has been developed, but after the planning stage, he or she welcomes information, particularly insofar as it supports the designated plan. The Planner derives emotional support and strength from a conviction of his or her usefulness, as a shaping influence, on disorderly projects and groups. To a degree, the Planner also derives emotional strength simply from the nature of the plan developed—its symmetry, scope, and interrelation of parts—no matter how events turn out.

Planners may experience speaker's nerves when time schedules collapse, promised resources go missing, and presentation venues suddenly change. Planners have difficulty adjusting to such changes. Their frustration can come out in the form of speaker's nerves: "This isn't how I wanted to develop the presentation. I don't think it's very good. My reputation will sink if I have to give a half-baked speech."

One solution to the Planner's risk of speaker's nerves is to develop a full-blown PowerPoint version of the presentation at hand. Even if the content has to be condensed due to unexpected and annoying schedule changes, the Planner can assure him- or herself, "They knew I had the complete package worked out, even though I didn't get to talk about all of it." After the presentation, the Planner will probably take the time to e-mail the PowerPoint slides to participants, so they can see once again how complete the preparation was.

T — Thinker

Someone with a Thinker personality is disposed toward finding, or attempting to find, logical links between thoughts, ideas, concepts, facts, details, and examples. The Thinker insists on postponing action until he or she figures out the underlying causes, effects, and relative accuracy or truth of propositions and assertions. When in a data-gathering mode, the Thinker is intent on knowing more, but when in assimilating and reasoning modes, the Thinker may reject or postpone new input of any kind. The Thinker derives emotional support and strength from the satisfaction of reaching logically defensible solutions to problems. Whether anyone acts on the basis of those solutions is less important to the Thinker than the success of the mental processes involved at arriving at them.

Thinkers may experience speaker's nerves if their audience requires a lighter, more general treatment of the topic than the Thinker wants to present: "I know my listeners are just store managers, but there's only one logical way to explain how the company's new inventory-tracking system works. It's a complicated explanation, but I'm not going to dumb it down. If I oversimplify it, I won't be entirely accurate. I'm nervous about going over the heads of my audience, but I'm more nervous about having to read some edited version of my speech that doesn't make good technological sense."

One solution to the Thinker's risk of speaker's nerves may lie in an extended question-and-answer session following the formal presentation. If the Thinker worries that the presentation itself merely skimmed the surface of the topic, he or she can calm down in the knowledge that more specific explanations, data, and examples can be provided during the Q & A.

E — Empathizer

Someone with an Empathizer personality is predisposed to focus on the emotional content of situations, as experienced personally or by others. The Empathizer appraises new information or a new situation first according to its emotional potential: How do I feel about this? How do others feel? Who will be hurt? Who will be happy? The answers to these questions play a prominent role in shaping the Empathizer's eventual point of view and action regarding the new information or situation. The Empathizer derives emotional support and strength from his or her self-image as a sensitive, caring individual and, often, from the gratitude and friendship of those targeted for his or her empathy.

Empathizers may experience speaker's nerves if asked or required to deliver a dry, fact-filled presentation that has no emotional appeal for the audience: "I can read the accounting presentation they gave me, but I'm going to feel extremely awkward doing so. Coming from a human resources background, I have the reputation in the company of building morale and encouraging people's efforts. I'm very nervous about giving a flat, boring presentation. People will think I've changed and that I don't care anymore."

One solution to the Empathizer's risk of speaker's nerves is to set the stage at the beginning of the presentation with a passionate statement of "why this all matters." The same kind of heartfelt appeal can conclude the speech. Those emotional bookends allow the Empathizer to feel more comfortable plowing through the bulk of a speech that he or she considers dry and boring.

C — Closer

An individual with a Closer personality is predisposed to make conclusions, judgments, and decisive acts, sometimes contrary to established procedures and rules. The Closer is generally impatient with delays urged by others for additional thought, research, or planning. The Closer often grants that the whole truth is not known but argues that enough of the truth is already available for adequate decision making. This personality type can be deaf to input that does not contribute directly to finalizing projects and processes. The Closer derives emotional support and strength from his or her reputation in the group as an action-oriented, no-nonsense decision maker and from the satisfaction of having used power, tolerance for risk, and a measure of daring to manage difficult problems and personalities.

The Closer may experience speaker's nerves when asked to give a presentation that does not lead to clear conclusions and immediate action steps: "They want me to talk at the convention about possible new directions for research and development in the company. That's way too foggy for me. I don't like to speculate about a bunch of what-ifs in the future. If they force me to make the speech, I will feel like a fish out of water."

One solution to the Closer's risk of speaker's nerves is to punctuate uncomfortably airy material with occasional bottom-line messages of the speaker's own creation: "I'm going to describe six company projects that may seem to be up in the clouds to you. But in each case, I'm going to conclude with a specific, concrete example of how the project may be able to become a new profit stream for the company."

R—Researcher

Someone with a Researcher personality is predisposed to postpone judgment and action as long as it is possible to acquire new information. The Researcher craves certainty and suspects conclusions reached without consideration of all the evidence. The Researcher frequently ignores time and resource constraints in pressing on with the search for additional data. In communicating the data to others, the Researcher may not be able to successfully organize and summarize the data gathered, since these activities involve drawing tentative conclusions. The Researcher derives emotional support and strength from the treasure hunt excitement of investigation, from the strong influence the findings have upon eventual planning, and from the other group members' admiration of his or her knowledge.

A Researcher may experience speaker's nerves when asked or required to give presentations comprising succinct summaries, specific predictions, and final results: "There's more to the story, and I'm not going to get up in front of people and pretend that we've answered all the questions. The truth is that we're rushing to judgment on a lot of these issues. If I'm the one who has to pretend otherwise in front of an audience, I'll do so kicking and screaming."

One solution to the Researcher's risk of speaker's nerves is to extend the boundaries of available information for the listeners. The Researcher does not rankle at giving partial information as long as he or she can say, "The complete data on this issue have been organized for you at a website I developed, www.morethanIwantedtoknow.com. I recommend that you visit the website right after my presentation to understand all the facts related to this important company development."

Appendix C

Six Practice Scripts for Enjoyable, Confident Speaking

THE FOLLOWING SHORT practice scripts can be used when working alone on speaking skills or with a speaking coach. Each vignette gives the speaker the chance to relax into the story, experiment with various moods and voices, and deliver the piece expressively and convincingly. Each script has a humorous aspect purposely included as an antidote against speaker's nerves. A speaker is less likely to be nervous knowing that audience members are delighted by what they are hearing.

Note: Each script can be presented by a man or a woman; simply pencil in pronoun changes to make the script yours.

Speech Script 1: Sports and Spitting

During the recent World Series, I could not help but notice that baseball players spit—a lot. By contrast, baseball fans do not spit. As the TV camera panned many thousands of cheering fans, I could spot only one spitter, an upchucking infant (with a future in professional baseball). So obnoxious was the spitting habit in the early days of the game that Judge Kenesaw Mountain Landis, baseball's first commissioner, decreed in 1921 that there would be "no expectorating on or along the sides of the baseball diamond." When spitting did not abate (but in fact doubled out of stubbornness), the angry judge demanded that "every team dig a latrine for spitters." Long latrines were promptly dug along the first base and third base lines of every professional field. Spitters, however, refused to use them. Apoplectic now, the judge ruled that "any player who spits must sit in the latrine when not otherwise engaged in play." He softened a bit by allowing team owners to call the latrines "dugouts" for marketing reasons.

Other sports managed to control spitting in ingenious ways. Professional football placed a face guard on every helmet, making spitting a self-punishing act. Spitters proud of their good aim through their face guards were fitted with mouth guards the size of an Idaho potato. They could not spit if they wanted to. Tennis required that players sweat profusely as a substitute for spitting. The net loss of fluid in a match, however, was allowed to be approximately the same, within a liter or two, for tennis players as for baseball players. Swimming allowed unrestricted spitting so long as the swimmer's face was beneath water. It is still common to see winners at swimming competitions dunk one last time for a spit before jumping out of the pool in triumph. The underwater rule did not apply to divers at first but became mandatory after unsightly occurrences during the triple somersault dives. Bikers and marathon runners may spit only into containers disguised as plastic water bottles, a clever PR ploy to make it seem that these athletes are drinking rather than spitting. Basketball players used to spit with the best of them until embarrassed team owners hit on the strategy of polishing the court to a high gloss. Any spit would send a player sliding head over heels. Hockey adopted a similar solution, requiring players to skate on polished ice. Hitting a spit bump cured even the most flagrant drooler.

America's youth are now spared exposure to unrestrained adult spitting by an FCC ruling in favor of so-called "dry" TV channels—those broadcasters whose screens go momentarily black when a spitting act seems imminent. (The telltale signs just before spitting, at least for baseball, are a slight puffing of the cheeks, a pursing of the lips, a hanging of the head, and a foolish look of unrepentant stupidity.) Fans watching "dry" channels complain that they miss at least half of every baseball game due to spit-outs, as they are called in the business. But at least the enthusiasm of children for America's game has not dampened.

Speech Script 2: The Wisdom of My Dog

Having observed my dog and his habits for twelve years, I believe I have achieved enlightenment. I don't compare my heights of wisdom to those attained by Buddha after his six years under the Bodhi tree, although it is worth pointing out that I've put in twice the hours. My revelation came in the form of nine principles. I had wished fervently for ten in order to align with the Ten Commandments, the ten months in the original Roman calendar, and *Ten*, the title of Pearl Jam's debut studio album in 1991. But alas, there were only nine, with no one of them so fat with insight that it could be split into two. Observing my dog for yet another year simply to achieve a total of ten principles seemed foolish, since the dog is getting old. At any rate, here are the Nine Principles, now capitalized, in the order they were revealed to me. I used Roman numerals to emphasize their gravity and importance, with no slight intended to Arabic numbers, which are also nice in the main and have a long, peaceful history in America. But I digress. The Nine Principles, please:

I. **Don't chase wild cats.**
   The problem lies not so much in the chasing, which can be fun, as in the catching. Once you have caught a wild cat, you face the lifelong problem of what to do with it.

II. **Sleep indoors whenever others will let you.**
   Often others may not want you to sleep indoors with them. You may have to bark to get in.

III. **Avoid the back room.**
   Veterinarians appear to be your friend until they take you into the back room. Do not willingly accompany anyone to a back room, especially a politician.

IV. **Consider sleep as the default position in life.**
   When not otherwise occupied, fall asleep right away. Others know to let you lie.

V. **Show appreciation for extra blessings.**
   Dry food can be tolerated with a yawn, but a ladle of gravy requires that you wag your tail or shake your booty, depending on your species.

VI. **Lick no man's hand.**
Hand-licking has been passé for decades; no self-respecting dog licks a hand that holds no food. Stay *au courant* in your obsequiousness.

VII. **Nip, don't bite.**
A nip holds the promise of a bite, but not its penalties. Nip early, nip often.

VIII. **Let no itch go unscratched.**
Actual or metaphorical, one's itches create an urgent agenda for daily activity. One's scratching, our mothers told us, only leads to further itching. As Simba would say, were he a dog, "the cycle of life."

IX. **Pursue every strange sound and smell.**
Curiosity killed the cat, but left the dog entirely unharmed, nose still out the car window, ears flapping in the breeze. Be the first in the home to discover what goes bump in the night or what smells like toast.

As for the symmetry of a final, tenth principle, the rest is silence. "The Moving Finger writes; and having writ, moves on," wrote the dog-lover Omar Khayyam. ". . . A bowl of chow and thou."

Speech Script 3: The Wedding Reception

Women have said "no" to me in many languages: "nej," "ne," "neen," "nein," "nyet," "nah," "nit," "nagoes," "iya," "lo," "mai," and "no." I am the United Nations of female rejection. Last week I attended a wedding reception, reputedly a good place to find someone "fair as a star when only one is shining in the sky," as Wordsworth wrote of his Lucy. The desired one approached me from across the room, as if with a purpose. I wore my recently acquired tux (eBay Armani, $42 plus shipping, no returns, dry cleaning definitely recommended) and, to my delight, so did she: stylish black satin slacks, a genderless tuxedo shirt, perky bow tie, and marvelous cuff links, with center stones that certainly were onyx, or at least a very high grade of plastic. Coyly, she pretended to walk past me unawares. "Miss, may I buy you a drink?"

"No." Her answer was curt, but lacked the hostility I had come to expect from women.

I tried wit. "But of course I can't. This is a wedding and drinks are free. Shall I get us drinks from the complimentary bar?"

Again, "no," and she began to move away.

I persisted, as my dating manuals suggested: "Am I correct in assuming that you don't drink?"

"No. Really." She stepped away.

"Wait," I called. "A point of clarification. Do you mean no, I'm not correct in my assumption that you don't drink, in which case you *do* drink, or no, you don't drink, in which case we should dance?" A master stroke, a checkmate in the game of love.

"Look, mister—" she began with a more determined look.

The "mister" fascinated me. How polite for a first meeting. Perhaps a Southern belle here, a faded debutante. I gently took her arm and tugged her a few feet to the crowded dance floor. She stood like a stone. "Let's crank," I suggested, referring to a youthful new dance I had recently learned from a YouTube video clip. I began my moves, a soul version of the Macarena with just the right hint of Fred Astaire. Her face was ashen. I cranked more furiously, trying to encourage her to move something.

"Are you—a friend—of—the bride—or—the groom?" I panted, crank, crank.

She mumbled something about "kate."

I shouted above the din, "You're Canadian? I have an aunt in Winnepeg!"

She roared back at the top of her lungs, "I'M THE CATERER!"

Three couples around us stopped dead in their tracks to look our way.

"Well!" I blew a long, silent whistle as I considered my limited options. I didn't want to quit dancing, suggesting some sort of class consciousness not unlike Prince Albert dropping his cigar ash in the cap of his valet. "Well, well!" I repeated, transitioning from the height of my cranking to a more legato version of the one-man rumba.

Then she spoke again. The dear saved me from antipopulist thoughts and celibacy ad infinitum: "I'm off at 10 if you want to get a cup of coffee."

Thirteen words, or twelve, if you count 10 as a number. A bouquet of words, a dozen sparkling diamonds of communication. My stars, I had a date! But what to wear. Would my Tommy Bahama "Born to Party" shirt opened to the third button send too sensual a message? Perhaps my eBay Hathaway, rolled twice at the cuff, $12, worn only twice, all buttons intact, from the mortuary in Iowa.

Speech Script 4: Privacy

I will handle this complaint with the greatest delicacy, as required by the FCC. It concerns door latches in the stalls of men's restrooms throughout the country. The fact is that, by my count, at least half of all such latches are missing, broken, or otherwise out of order. I won't presume to speak for latches in women's restrooms, which I have not investigated with any particular thoroughness. The latch problem hinges not so much on keeping the occupant in as keeping intruders out. Faced with an unlatched door, how does one signal "Taken" to the waiting world? Yao Ming may be able to stick a foot out under the door from a seated position, but such contortions are impossible for the rest of us. An empty shoe set in view bespeaks an unacceptable settling in with regard to the stall space — permanent residency rather than temporary visitation. Similarly, a necktie draped from the door attracts rather than repels the curious.

When I last encountered the dilemma of the unlatchable stall, I decided to hum a tune loud enough for any would-be barger to hear and heed. But what song? I began with a bar or two of "People, People Who Need People" but stopped before the melody exceeded my range. Exiting Streisand, I also found that most of my Barry Manilow repertoire seemed somehow inappropriate for the moment. I needed a song — just a ditty really — that seemed purposeless and entirely idle but nevertheless made my human presence unmistakably known. But I certainly didn't want to appear to be entertaining myself or attempting to entertain anyone else. Inspiring others to clap along was hardly my aim. And I didn't feel comfortable with a "message" song like anything from "Sound of Music" —

"the hills are alive," indeed!—and who can hum anything from "Rent" or "Wicked"? I settled on some vintage Kenny Rogers, putting a bit of extra emphasis for any potential intruder on "know when to walk away, and when to run." I intended my rendition to conjure up a foul-tempered gambling man, derringer in hand, who was not to be disturbed. It worked. Between phrases I heard the shuffle of footsteps toward my door, the pause of recognition, and the welcome retreat. I've used the song many times since with almost uniform success, except for one autograph seeker.

Speech Script 5: Empty Police Cars

You've no doubt noticed the empty police cars parked at notorious trouble spots around town. A speeder rounds the corner only to hit the brakes when he sees the black-and-white. Well under the speed limit now, he innocently passes the police car only to notice that it has no constabulary occupant. Fool me once. The next day he speeds around the corner again and, from force of habit, hits the brakes again when he sees the police car—empty, dagnab it! Fool me twice. The third day he roars around the corner, speeds right past the police car, and gives it a long blast on the horn to say "you can't fool me three times!" He looks back in his rearview mirror to see—uh-oh—the officer's head rising above the seat. (The officer had assumed what in law enforcement is technically called the "napping position" across the front seat as a strategy to surprise speeders.) The scofflaw was promptly ticketed.

Empty police cars are part of a statewide law enforcement program called SOFA (Show of Force Alternative). Officers position their empty cars around town, freeing themselves (after a cab ride back to the station) for additional time on the SOFA (program). The genesis of the program has an interesting human side. The wife of a police chief in a far away city (note: not our police chief, not his wife, not his city) in a far away state wanted to make sure that his evening activities at the upcoming State Police Convention were, shall we say, without companionship. She couldn't accompany him on the trip to monitor his behavior. But she came up with a brilliant stratagem to make him, well, hit the brakes. The night before he left for the convention she placed the business card of a local private investigator on his night table. Nothing was said. Nothing needed to be said.

Chastened and warned by the card, the police chief went to the convention with a bright idea of his own (replacing the other bright ideas he had contemplated prior to seeing the card). "We don't need to be on the scene ourselves," he told his fellow conventioneers. "We just have to appear to be on the scene by parking our cars here and there." The applause was deafening, but not so much so as to squelch a couple good questions: "Chief, how will we leave the station without cars?" The chief explained that they could all ride in the one car left at the station. He showed them an old *Keystone Cops* movie to illustrate the idea. "Chief, won't crooks catch on that our cars are empty?" That question, a puzzler at the moment, led to a study grant from the SOFA program to measure the intelligence of criminals and the practicality of cardboard heads placed in empty police cars. The cardboard heads were nixed by the Police Union, unless they paid dues.

Since that time, empty police cars dot our streets, maintaining their 24/7 vigil against crime. Not to be outdone by this amplified police presence, the substantial criminal element in our midst has struck back with a ploy of its own. Now a lone criminal stands across the street from the empty police car. Just as the car reminds citizens of protection, the silent, solitary crook reminds passers-by of threat. It's tit for tat.

The police chief (not ours, remember), ever a fountain of creative law enforcement ideas, struck on another brilliant plan last week. He approached the lone criminal sentinel standing across the street from one of the empty police cars with a proposition. "Look," the chief said, "you're standing out here in the cold and the rain. I've got an empty car over there that isn't doing much since everyone knows it's empty. Let's combine our talents. You sit in the car. In fact, here, wear this police cap. You get out of the cold and we get a car that looks like it's occupied." The lion and the lamb lie down together, as Blake wrote. Solution sweet. The plan got even better when the police chief hit on the idea of driving the criminal in the car to the jail—or, actually, letting him drive himself there, since he was sitting in the driver's seat. The charge: impersonating a police officer.

Speech Script 6: Eyeglasses

"Where are my glasses?" I must say that fifty times a week. My spouse is no gem when she answers, "Look in the bedroom." I can't see the bedroom. I don't have my glasses. "Get some neck straps," she urges, in that same semisweet tone she used to nix my modest, fully clothed bachelor party thirty years ago. I'll get you a neck strap, sister. A big one. Besides, those neck straps don't help. They keep getting tangled up in my Medic Alert necklace and yanking my head down on my chest. In fact, my Medic Alert tag says, "This patient is subject to sudden strangulation from eyeglass neck straps." On the other side of the tag is the 800-number of a Boy Scout who is good at untying knots. No, that's not the truth. That's eyeglass humor. The real truth is that I don't know what my Medic Alert tag says. I can't read it—because I don't have my glasses. I can feel the big letters with my thumb, and they either say I have "Diabetes" or "Diarrhea." In either case, it's serious and worth alerting someone (though apparently not my wife, neck strap woman). I hope the near-sighted paramedic who finds me laid out half under the bed (looking for you-know-what) has a more considerate spouse than I do. I can see him now on his emergency radio: "Base station, I don't have my glasses, but I think this guy has Delirium or Delphinium. I can't quite make out his Medic Alert tag. It's all tangled up with the neck strap on his glasses. He's turning blue." Look in the bedroom indeed. *She* could look in the bedroom. *She* could make sure my glasses find their way into a neat little tray on my night table the same way her glasses always migrate to her neat little tray on her night table. But no. On the issue of glasses my otherwise penurious bride is a wild woman: "Just buy several pairs and put them around the house. They're cheap enough." First, I don't call $11.95 cheap. Cheapish, but not cheap. Second, I feel like an idiot at the checkout buying five pairs of reading specs. The checker knows exactly what I'm doing but pretends not to: "Shopping for friends? Earthquake preparedness for the home?" Right, five friends who mysteriously all wear 3.25 magnification glasses. I manage a weak, "touché" smile in her fuzzy, blobbish direction (remember, I have no glasses at this point, though I'm getting close) and answer, "Yeah, cut the tag off one pair. I'll wear them out of the store. The others are for my wife, blind old bat." Five pairs of cheap readers will last me a week if I'm lucky. I don't know where they go. Some immediately slide out of the little plastic bag onto the car seat and down into that irretrievable, skin-your-fingers crack between the seats. Others break within a day or two. The over-the-ear side things (What are they called? Arms? Legs?) break off when I bend them ever so slightly to accommodate my ample head. I don't try to fix them by wrapping tape around and around to hold the glasses together. Saw the taped look on a kid in high school physics class. Didn't like it then, don't like it now. So I'm left with armless, legless pince-nez remnants that I squeeze, Louis-like, onto the most bulbous part of my otherwise attractive though somewhat oily nose. For about twenty seconds. Then they slip off, fall to the floor, and disappear into the haze at my feet. Or behind me, if they bounced. I would look for them, but I—you can finish the sentence.

Appendix D

Working with a Speech Coach

LET'S MAKE A few assumptions:

1. You've assured yourself, with the help of your medical professional, that your symptoms of speaker's nerves aren't caused by physical ills or deep-seated emotional problems. You have performance jitters, plain and simple.
2. You've tried to "go it alone" in making progress with regard to speaker's nerves. Nothing works to your satisfaction.
3. You decide that you need one-on-one or small group assistance with the specifics of presentations—the dozens of little tricks and techniques that can increase your comfort, calm your anxieties, and amplify your impact with your audience.

That's where a speech coach comes in.

These men and women, fortunately, are to be found throughout the country, usually at relatively affordable prices compared to other one-on-one professionals, such as lawyers, psychologists, and financial advisors. The coaches listed at the end of this appendix should be considered as resources for investigation, not as recommendations. In addition to these professionals, you can often find an expert, affordable speech coach through your local university, college, or community college. These individuals can be located most often by contacting the communication department of these schools and asking to be put in touch with a faculty member who teaches public speaking. Many of these professors consult as speech coaches "on the side," and often at more attractive rates due to their lower overhead expenses. You may decide to take a class in public speaking instead of or in addition to your individual coaching.

Who a Speech Coach Is

Speech coaches come from many backgrounds. Some have academic degrees in communication, rhetoric, or dramatic arts. Others learned their speaking skills through extracurricular competition in college debate, oratory, extemporaneous speaking, and dramatic interpretative reading. Still others came from a human resources background and found themselves teaching presentation skills in corporate training programs. Then there are the "black sheep" of the speech coaching industry: those individuals with no formal training, who perhaps have given a few rousing speeches at civic organizations and, voila, consider themselves qualified to teach others. Although some of the people in this last category may be gifted mentors, they generally share the common flaw of teaching others to "speak like me." Lacking broad training in public speaking, they often have only one model by which to evaluate and coach others: their own speaking style.

Bona fide speech coaches can often be recognized by their membership in national and international associations devoted to the deeper understanding and improvement of instruction in public speaking. These include, but are not limited to, the National Speakers Association, the National Communication Association, the Association for Business Communication, the Canadian Association of Professional Speakers, the American Seminar Leaders Association, Toastmasters International, the International Communication Association, the Media Communication Association, the International Association of Business Communicators, the Speech Association of America, the Association for Women in Communications, and the International Speech Communication Association. (Some of these organizations have a primary focus on the scientific study of human speech.) "Certified Speaking Professional" (CSP) is the highest earned designation awarded by the National Speakers Association. Another designation achieved by some speech coaches is the Accredited Public Relations (APR) credential given by the Universal Accreditation Board. Master's and Ph.D. degrees in relevant speech fields are also strong evidence of professional qualification.

Like a college sports coach, the speech coach may no longer be an "active athlete" in terms of giving regular speeches. However, she should have more than an academic knowledge of public speaking and the anxieties that often accompany it. Virtually all successful speech coaches have extensive experience at the podium themselves. They can therefore relate on an emotional as well as intellectual level to what their students are going through.

What a Speech Coach Does

Although speech coaching takes many forms depending on individual needs, the process usually involves at least eight activities on the coach's part, not necessarily in this order.

Listening

A good speech coach makes no assumptions about what a new student wants or needs. The coach does not impose the learning paths of previous students on the new student. Instead, he listens carefully and empathetically to what the student says about speaking experiences to date: what went right or wrong, what symptoms of speaker's nerves occurred, how the student felt about particular presentations, and what barriers the student wants to overcome.

Assessing

Often a student's self-described problems with public speaking are only the tip of the iceberg when it comes to an accurate picture of her speaking competence. The speech coach devises several opportunities to see the student "in action" and, based on that evidence, draws together a thorough assessment of the student's strengths and weaknesses as a presenter. This assessment should be "observable and preservable"—written down in an organized way (perhaps using an assessment form) that can be referred to throughout the coaching process. Verbal assessment alone can too easily be forgotten or ignored.

Establishing Goals

The speech coach and student use the initial assessment to establish learning goals, including an approximate time line for achieving those goals. Topic areas for goals can include:

- Progressive reduction in bothersome nervous symptoms
- Increased confidence and comfort in front of audiences of various sizes
- Improved use of gestures, eye contact, pace, pauses, and voice qualities
- Enhanced skills in the use of succinct, specific language
- Better use of high-interest presentation components such as anecdotes, headlines, humor, and visual aids
- Improved organization of speech parts
- Reduced reliance on speaking notes
- Stronger speech beginnings and endings
- More skillful handling of "Q & A" during and after presentations

Strategizing

Once goals have been agreed on between coach and student, the process of mapping out a strategy for achieving those goals begins. Few coaches delineate a complete strategy for all goals from the outset. More often, coach and student select one or two initial goals and strategize for their achievement. Based on how those strategies succeed, the process is then continued, often with adjustments, for the remaining goals.

It's crucial that these strategies are shared with the student. A coach should never leave the student in the awkward position of saying or feeling, "I don't know why he's making me do this, but I guess he has some plan in mind."

Practicing

When goals and initial strategies are established, the real work of improvement takes place through guided practice. This process usually involves many stops and starts, as the student tries out various techniques, tricks of the trade, and alternative approaches suggested by the speech coach. The practice portion of any coaching relationship usually takes up the majority of training time.

Providing Feedback

Students naturally want to know "how am I doing?" Skilled coaches not only give their opinion on progress, but also involve the student in realistic self-assessment. A coach might say, for example, "Tell me how that speaking experience felt" or "You seemed less nervous that time—what made the difference?"

Encouraging

Throughout the coaching experience, the student receives much more encouragement than negative criticism. Speech coaches try to build on an individual student's strengths as a way of increasing self-confidence and the desire to tackle increasingly challenging speech barriers.

Empowering

At the same time that a speech coach tries to make herself intimately aware of a student's speech issues, the speech coach also works toward the time when the student can break free from the coach's support and supervision—"leaving the nest," as it were, to fly on one's own. The Confucian wisdom regarding true leadership applies well to coaching: "Of the best leader, the people said 'we did it ourselves.'"

Questions to Ask a Potential Speech Coach

Choosing a speech coach is not unlike selecting a personal physician. You want to make sure that you relate well to the individual and trust his expertise and methods. The following questions can be useful conversation starters as you interview prospective speech coaches. Asking all these questions, of course, would be overkill. Select the ones that matter most to you in making the right choice of a coach for your specific needs and goals.

Tell me about your professional credentials, including speeches you've given.
Some people are embarrassed to ask this kind of "qualifying" question. Don't be. Bona fide speech coaches are happy to discuss their professional background, much as a sports coach expects to answer questions about win-loss records and coaching philosophy.

How long have you been a speech coach?
Longevity in the speech coaching field does not guarantee excellence, but it does give you a general idea of how the coach's work has been received by others over time and the variety of individuals she has worked with. If you are the coach's first student, you deserve to know before signing on to the expense and commitment of the relationship.

How many presenters have you worked with individually? In class settings?
Speech coaches may be vague or expansive about their numbers of past students: "Oh, I've worked with hundreds of speakers in the past decade." It's worthwhile to probe exactly what such claims mean. For example, did the coach teach a few large sections of Public Speaking 101 at a local college? If so, is she counting those students among the "hundreds" of her clients? Get a clear picture of a prospective coach's number of one-on-one client relationships before signing on the dotted line.

Describe the levels of company responsibility among your past clients? Entry-level workers? Supervisors? Managers? Executives? Top company leaders and CEOs?

A speech coach should be forthcoming in telling you exactly what levels of employees he has worked with over the years, and in what approximate percentage. If you are a mid-level manager attempting to improve your presentation skills with an eye toward promotion, you may not want to sign on with a coach who has only worked with entry-level workers or college freshmen.

Do you require a contract of some kind? A minimum number of sessions? How much notice must I give to end our work together?

Some coaches prefer a pay-as-you-go fee structure, where every session is billed on an hourly basis, allowing the student to quit the relationship at any time. Others arrange a retainer, against which hourly charges are billed. Still others have a staged payment system in which the student pays for coaching in blocks of time tied to mutually agreed on goals. No matter what the payment scheme, it's wise to "get it in writing" to prevent misunderstandings.

Can you provide references of other presenters you've helped with speaker's nerves?

Speech coaches rarely open their entire record of past clients, especially since assistance with speaker's nerves is not something that all students want to reveal to the world. But it should be a red flag to any coaching relationship if the coach cannot produce a single client willing to serve as a reference. Typically, a successful speech coach will be able to give you a referral list of several past clients who are willing to speak with you about their experience with the coach.

Have you ever experienced speaker's nerves? How did you handle the problem?

Ideally, the speech coach will bring his own experience to the table in working with you on speaker's nerves and other presentation issues. It can be both reassuring and encouraging to know that you are being coached by an individual who has faced and overcome the speaking obstacles that you are confronting.

Tell me about your coaching method.
You wouldn't give a realtor the listing to sell your home without having a clear idea of what she planned to do in marketing it. In the same way, you need to understand what to expect from your coach. Will she talk you to death? Will the coach always expect you to imitate her speaking behavior? Will the coach nitpick at trivial items (for example, the number of um's in your speech)? These are matters best sorted out before committing to a coaching relationship.

What do you think causes speaker's nerves?
This can be a good litmus test question for the prospective speech coach's depth of knowledge and understanding. If he says, "It's nothing—just ignore it," you have good reason to keep looking for a qualified coach.

What's your success rate in working with people who suffer from speaker's nerves?
In choosing a surgeon for any medical procedure, you would certainly ask about the rate of favorable outcomes. A speech coach should be able to provide a good estimate of how well her methods work with those who suffer from speech anxiety in its various forms.

How often should we meet?
Your commitment to a speech coach involves more than money. Some coaches will expect to meet several times per month or even per week. You need to know (and perhaps negotiate) the kind of time schedule that the coach expects.

What takes place in a typical meeting?
A speech coach should be able to talk you through a typical session, including how long it will last, what you will be expected to do in preparation for the session, and what kinds of activities you will be doing during the session.

Does one session build on the previous session? If so, how?
You need to know in advance if every session will be the same (like playing scales endlessly for a piano teacher) or whether sessions are designed in a progressive way to build on one another.

Tell me about the kinds of resources you use (DVDs, printed materials, audio tapes, etc.).
Entire sections of some large libraries are devoted to public speaking and human communication learning materials. Does the prospective speaking coach make use of some of these valuable materials in his coaching?

Will you be available to observe my actual presentations?
The policies of speech coaches vary widely on this issue. Some are willing to travel to your workplace to observe and evaluate a particular speech as part of their coaching work with you. Others avoid such on-site work or attach a hefty surcharge for seeing you in action as a speaker at work. Know the policy of your coach in advance.

What are your feelings about videotaping my practice presentations?
Some coaches make extensive use of videotaping, with virtually every speech you give being recorded and analyzed. Other coaches reserve videotape for the "dress rehearsal" or final presentation of a speech you may have worked on for weeks. You may have strong feelings about being recorded and watching yourself on tape. Discuss this matter in advance with your coach.

Can you show me an example of the typical kind of written feedback you give?
After paying a retainer to a speech coach, some students are disappointed to learn that she simply provides a checklist or point score as feedback after presentations. If you want more than a series of check marks to indicate your progress, ask to see the kind of written feedback your prospective coach provides for students.

Is confidentiality assured, including any unauthorized use of my practice videos or reference to me by name or general description in your advertising or conversation with other clients?

If you have a successful experience with your speaking coach, you may decide to give him permission to include your name as a reference for other students. But you certainly will want to control where and how your name is used—and where your practice videotapes may end up. More than one student speaker has been embarrassed to see her shakiest moments as a public speaker made available to millions on YouTube. Clarify in writing with your coach the confidentiality that you expect as part of the coaching relationship.

At what location do you prefer to meet? Why?

This detail of the coaching experience can become a major source of irritation if the coach expects to use your home or place of work as the primary location for coaching sessions—complete with snacks and drinks. Even if you are comfortable meeting in your own space, iron out the specifics of this issue in advance.

Do you have different methods and goals for female speakers vs. male speakers? Please explain.

Some coaches have rigid ideas of "how men should present" vs. "how women should present." You won't know how your prospective coach feels about this issue unless you ask.

Are you familiar with common presentation technologies (PowerPoint, Director, etc.)? Can you teach me how to use these technologies effectively?

We have all observed disastrous presentations that went astray more because of electronic incompetence or bad luck than because of poor speaking skills. If your presentations will involve media in one form or another, choose a speaking coach deeply familiar with these technologies and their optimal use.

How do you feel about memorizing a speech word for word?
This question can be another useful litmus test for prospective speech coaches. You may want to think twice about any coach who tells you "all successful speeches are completely memorized."

Are you set up to work remotely using Skype, iChat, or another audiovisual connection?
In the coaching relationship, it's often unnecessary to send our bodies where only our minds and images need to go. Does your coach know how to use Internet audiovisual connections so that you can participate in a remote practice session or one that focuses on speaking skills used in teleconferencing?

Where to Find a Speech Coach

The following list of speech coaches is current to press time for this book. These individuals and organizations should be considered as resources for your exploration, not as referrals. They are listed in alphabetical order according to the first keyword in their company name.

Art Bell, Business and Professional Speech Coaching
www.artbellspeechcoach.blogspot.com

Arvee Robinson's InstantProSpeaker.com
www.instantprospeaker.com

Baldoni Consulting L.L.C.
www.baldoniconsulting.com

Better Accent Tutor for English
www.betteraccent.com

CCG: Comm Core Consulting Group
www.CommCoreConsulting.com

Communispond
www.communispond.com

Executive Speech Coach
www.executivespeechcoach.blogspot.com

Fresh Eyes Consulting
www.fresheyesconsultants.com

Fripp
www.fripp.com

George Torok: SpeechCoachforExecutives.com
www.speechcoachforexecutives.com

Jan D'Arcy
www.jdarcy.com

Katina Kalin, Speech & Voice Coach
www.katinakalin.com

Linda Hearne, High Impact Coaching
www.High-Impact-Coaching.com

Lindsay Strand Associates
www.lindsaystrand.com

Margaret Hope
www.lionsgatetraining.com

Marian K. Woodall Communications for Professionals
www.speechdoctor.com

Mitchell Friedman Communications
www.mitchellfriedman.com

More Than Speaking
www.morethanspeaking.com

Podium Master
www.podiummaster.com

Sandra Schrift
www.schrift.com

Silicon Valley Speech Coach
www.siliconvalleyspeechcoach.com

SimplySpeaking.com
www.simplyspeakinginc.com

SNP Communications
www.snpnet.com

Speak for Yourself
www.speakforyourself.com

Speech and Voice Enterprises
www.speechandvoice.com

SpeechCoach.net
www.speechcoach.net

Speech-Coach
www.speech-coach.net

SpeechesNow.com
www.speechesnow.com

Straight Talk Announcing
www.yourvoiceprofessor.com

The Art of Speaking
www.sandrakazan.com

The Passionate Speaker
www.coachmike.com

The Speaking Bridge
www.thespeakingbridge.com

Voice Power Studios
www.voicepowerstudios.com

Voicepower
www.voicepowr.com [sic]

Wheless-Wyatt Communications
www.wheless-wyatt.com

Witt Communications
www.wittcom.com

Appendix E

General Speaking Guidelines

THE FOLLOWING LIST of dos and don'ts in public speaking can be useful in at least three ways. First, you can use these categories to remind yourself of the "must-have" qualities for virtually all public speaking, whether in business, civic life, social clubs, or elsewhere. Second, your speech coach can refer to these ten areas of speaking competence in giving you feedback. Finally, the list can serve as a "growth chart" of sorts, allowing you to check off aspects of public speaking you've mastered and target those you still need to work on.

Oral Presentations

1. **Speak up.**
   Audiences resent having to lean forward in an effort to catch your words.
2. **Achieve rapport quickly.**
   Use the first few moments to orient audience members and show you feel comfortable with them.
3. **Look at your listeners.**
   Indicate by your eye contact that you are talking with your listeners, not at them (or, worse, to the ceiling, floor, or walls).

4. **Use gestures to express your ideas.**
   Appropriate hand gestures and facial expressions add energy and communicate sincerity.
5. **Move freely, without pacing.**
   Use the available space to move naturally.
6. **Use notes (if necessary) as unobtrusively as possible.**
   Notes function as "thought triggers," not as verbatim transcripts.
7. **Highlight key ideas.**
   Voice volume, pauses, graphic aids, and "headlining" (tell listeners that a point is especially important) can all be used to emphasize key points.
8. **Channel nervous energy into an enthusiastic delivery.**
   Accept nerves as a natural form of excitement and use that energy to deliver your points with appropriate passion.
9. **Watch your audience for signs of comprehension or misunderstanding.**
   True communication is not a one-way lecture. Pay attention to the facial expressions and body language of audience members to determine if you're "getting through."
10. **End with a bang, not a whimper.**
    Your concluding words should be memorable for your listeners.

Bibliography

Atwood, T. 2004. *Exploring Feelings: Cognitive Behavior Therapy to Manage Anxiety*. Arlington, TX: Future Horizons Press.

Bandelow, B., et al. 2004. *Social Anxiety Disorder*. New York: Informa Healthcare.

Bell, A. and D. Smith. 2007. *Business Communication*. New York: Wiley & Sons.

———. 2006. *Management Communication*, 2nd ed. New York: Wiley & Sons.

Brogan, S. 2006. *Your Business Speech*. Kalamazoo, MI: Fidlar Doubleday.

Call, A. 2004. *Nerves and Common Sense*. Kila, MT: Kessinger Publishing.

DeWit, D. J., et al. "Antecedents of the Risk of Recovery from DSM-III-R Social Phobia." *Psychological Medicine* 29 (1999): 569–82.

Dowling, C. 1993. *You Mean I Don't Have to Feel This Way?* New York: Bantam.

Dwyer, K. 2004. *Conquer Your Speech Anxiety*. Belmont, CA: Wadsworth.

Essau, C. A., et al. "Frequency and Comorbidity of Social Phobia and Social Fears in Adolescents." *Behavioral Therapy* 37 (1999): 831–43.

Evans, R. "Communicative Competence as a Dimension of Shyness." In *Social Withdrawal, Inhibition, and Shyness in Childhood*, edited by J. Rubin et al., 189–212. Hillsdale, NJ: Lawrence Erlbaum, 1993.

Farnbach, R., et al. 2001. *Overcoming Performance Anxiety.* New York: Simon & Schuster.

Gardner, J., and A. Bell. 2001. *Overcoming Anxiety, Panic, and Depression.* Franklin Lakes, NJ: Career Press.

———. 2005. *Phobias and How to Overcome Them.* Franklin Lakes, NJ: Career Press.

Ginsburg, A., et al. "Social Anxiety in Children With Anxiety Disorders: Relation With Social and Emotional Functioning." *Journal of Abnormal Psychology* 26 (1998): 175–85.

Graham, P. and R. Juvonen. "Self-Blame and Peer Victimization in Middle School: An Attributional Analysis." *Developmental Psychology* 34 (1998): 587–99.

Hoff, R. 1997. *Do Not Go Naked into Your Next Presentation.* Kansas City, KS: Andrews & McMeel Publishing.

Hopf, T. 1993. *Coping with Speech Anxiety.* Norwood, NJ: Ablex Publishing.

Hunt, E. 2003. *Nerve Control.* Kila, MT: Kessinger Publishing.

Jung, C. G. *The Undiscovered Self.* First pub. 1957. Princeton, NJ: Princeton University Press, 1990.

Kendler, K. S., et al. "Fears and Phobias: Reliability and Heritability." *Psychological Medicine* 29 (1999): 529–53.

Krasne, M. 1997. *Say It with Confidence.* New York: Warner Books.

Leary, M., et al. 2006. *Social Anxiety.* New York: Guilford Press.

Lerner, H. 2004. *Fear and Other Uninvited Guests.* New York: HarperCollins.

Lieb, R., et al. "Parental Psychopathology, Parenting Styles, and the Risk of Social Phobia in Offspring." *Archives of General Psychiatry* 177 (2000): 859–66.

Luciani, J. 2001. *Self-Coaching: How to Heal Anxiety and Depression.* New York: Wiley & Sons.

Markway, B., et al. 1992. *Dying of Embarrassment: Help for Social Anxiety and Phobia.* Oakland, CA: New Harbinger Press.

McManus, J. 2002. *How to Write and Deliver Effective Speeches*. New York: Arco Publishing.

Morgan, N. 2005. *Give Your Speech, Change the World*. Cambridge, MA: Harvard Business School Press.

Neal-Barrett, A. 2003. *Soothe Your Nerves*. New York: Fireside Publishers.

Nohawk, A. 2004. *Power Speaking*. New York: Allworth Press.

Ost, R. "Ways of Acquiring Phobias and Outcome of Behavioral Treatments." *Behavior Research and Therapy* 23 (1985): 683–89.

Rapee, R. and H. Heimberg. "A Cognitive-Behavioral Model of Anxiety in Social Phobia." *Behavior Research and Therapy* 35 (1997): 741–56.

Schneier, F. R., et al. "Social Phobia: Comorbidity and Morbidity in an Epidemiological Sample." *Archives of General Psychiatry* 49 (1992): 282–88.

Sprague, J. 2005. *The Speaker's Handbook*. Belmont, CA: Wadsworth.

Stein, M. B., et al. "A Direct Interview Family Study of Generalized Social Phobia." *American Journal of Psychiatry* 155 (1998): 90–97.

Stemberg, J., et al. "Social Phobia: An Analysis of Possible Developmental Factors." *Journal of Abnormal Psychology* 104 (1995): 526–31.

Walters, L. 2000. *Secrets of Superstar Speakers*. New York: McGraw-Hill.

Weinstock, L. S. "Gender Differences in the Presentation and Management of Social Anxiety Disorder." *Journal of Clinical Psychiatry* 60 (supplement 9) (1999): 9–13.

Index

About the Author

ART BELL (www.artbellspeechcoach.blogspot.com) holds his Ph.D. in English from Harvard University and is Professor of Management Communication and Director of Program Strategy at the Masagung Graduate School of Management, University of San Francisco. He simultaneously holds the position of Research Professor, Department of Information Sciences, Naval Postgraduate School, Monterey, California, where he works on homeland security issues. Previously, he held teaching positions in the business schools and English departments at Georgetown University and the University of Southern California. He is a member of the National Speakers Association, Association for Business Communication, ASCAP, and Authors Guild.

Art is a prominent speech coach and seminar leader who has worked with managers, executives, and corporate leaders at dozens of organizations, including Charles Schwab, Wells Fargo, Citibank, American Stores, the U.S. Navy, TRW, Deutsche Telekom, Safeway, Cisco, Sun Microsystems, PriceWaterhouse Coopers, Cost Plus World Market, the U.S. State Department, British Telecomm, and IBM.

Among his most recent books are *Business Communication* (Wiley, 2007), *Management Communication* 3rd edition (Wiley, 2008), *Phobias and How to Overcome Them* (Career Press, 2005), *Overcoming Anxiety, Panic, and Depression* (Career Press, 2000), *Winning with Truth in Busi-*

ness (Pelican, 2008), and *You Can't Talk to Me That Way! Stopping Verbal Abuse at Work* (Career Press, 2007). He is also the author of *Resolving Conflict at Work* (2008), a corporate training film from Kantola Productions. In addition, Art is director of leadership thinking of SNP Communications, San Francisco, where he heads a think-tank focused on emerging communication and marketing issues and technologies.

He lives in Belvedere, California, with his wife, Dayle (also a business professor), and his two daughters.